DELICIOUSLY HEALTHY BAKING

BY AVNER LASKIN

President and Chief Executive Officer: Rick Barton
Vice President of Editorial: Susan White Sullivan
Vice President of Sales: Mike Behar
Vice President of Operations: Jim Dittrich
Vice President of Finance: Laticia Mull Dittrich
Vice President of Purchasing: Fred F. Pruss
National Sales Director: Martha Adams
Creative Services: Chaska Lucas
Information Technology Director: Hermine Linz
Controller: Francis Caple
Retail Customer Service Manager: Stan Raynor
Director of Designer Relations: Cheryl Johnson
Special Projects Director: Susan Frantz Wiles
Art Publications Director: Rhonda Shelby
Director of eCommerce-Prepress Services: Mark Hawkins

Produced for Leisure Arts, Inc. by Penn Publishing Ltd.
www.penn.co.il
Editor-in-Chief: Rachel Penn
Culinary editor: Tamar Zakut
Editor: Sebastia Richter
Design and layout: Studio Michal & Dekel
Photography: Danya Weiner
Styling: Orya Geva

PRINTED IN CHINA
ISBN-13: 978-1-60900-403-3
Library of Congress Control Number: 2011934410

Cover photography by Danya Weiner

DELICIOUSLY HEALTHY BAKING

BY
AVNER LASKIN

TABLE OF CONTENTS

INTRODUCTION   9

The Baker's Tools   11
Ingredients   13
Dark Sourdough Starter   19
White Sourdough Starter   20
The Baker's Techniques   21
Baking Tips   25

HOMEMADE HEALTHY   28
MORNING PASTRIES

Rye & Olive Breadsticks   31
Milk & Honey Mini-Rolls   32
Savory Breadsticks   34
Long & Twisted Whole-Grain Breadsticks   36
Spiced Breadsticks with Poppy Seeds   40
Crunchy Sesame Bagels   43
Breadsticks with Tomatoes & Herbs   44
Savory Whole-Grain Pastry   46
Rye Breadsticks with Cheese   48
Special Whole-Grain Rolls   49
Caramel-Pecan Buns   50
Pistachio & Brown Sugar Feast   53
Danish-Style Cheese Pocket & Cherry Pastry   56
Healthy Whole-Wheat Carrot Pastry   59

¤ *Rich Olive Bread (see page 100)*

EXTRAORDINARY BREADS FOR ORDINARY DAYS — 60

Aromatic Herb Bread — 63
Healthy Focaccia — 64
Classic Braided Shabbat Challah — 68
Country Rye Bread — 70
Whole-Wheat Bread with Flax Seeds — 71
Healthy-Harvest Grain Bread — 73
Two-Color Herb Bread — 75
Indulgent Dark Chocolate Sourdough Bread — 77
Worker's Dark Bread — 81
French-Style Country Bread — 82
Parmesan Rolls — 84
Hearty Rye Bread with Dried Fruit — 85
Dark Classic Country Baguettes — 86
Mediterranean Sesame-Coated Bread — 88
Classic Rye Bagels — 91
Beet & Anise Bread — 93
Sweet Anise-Scented Baguettes — 94
Zesty Roasted Corn & Chili Bread — Ciabatta Style — 96
Flavorful Mediterranean Bagels — 99
Rich Olive Bread — 100
Seeded Classic Ciabatta — 102
Sweet Chili & Cilantro Bread — 104
Three-Color Sesame Rolls — 105

SPECIAL BREADS — 106

Italian Walnut Bread — 109
Whole-Grain Carrot Bread — 110
Earthy Seed Loaf — 112
Decadent Fig & Goat Cheese Stuffed Bread — 114
Yellow Cheese & Wild Mushroom Bread — 115
Spiced Cheese & Nut Bread — 117
Prune & Port Whole-Wheat Bread — 118
Classic German Rye Bread — 120
Unique Wintry Chestnut Bread — 122
Honey-Lemon Bread — 123
Hazelnut Bread — 125
Country Bread with Wakame Seaweed — 126
Eggplant & Caciotta Cheese Bread — 128
Garlic Confit Focaccia — 131
Whole-Wheat Dried Fruit Bread — 132
Delicious Pumpkin-Raisin Bread — 134

HEALTHY CAKES 136

Delicious Whole-Wheat Carrot Muffins 139
Granola Loaf 140
Pizza with Green Apple & Emmental Swiss Cheese 142
Whole-Wheat Dried Fruit Cake 144
Natural Whole-Wheat Date Cake 145
Elegant Pear & Brown Sugar Pastry Topped with Pear Fan 147
Happy Honey Rye Cake 149
Baked Snacks with Cranberries & Oats 150
Decadent Dark Chocolate Loaf 153
Cherry Cake 154
Summery Apricot Cake 155
Exotic Pumpkin Marsala Mini-Cakes 156
Orange Kugelhopf Cake 158

POWER COOKIES 160

Savory Cheese Cookies 163
Fruity Granola Energy Cookies 164
Rich Granola & Dark Chocolate Cookies 167
Whole-Wheat Chocolate Cookies 168
Whole-Wheat Tahini Cookies 170
Caramel Mini-Cookies with Toasted Hazelnuts 173
Brown Sugar Nut Cookies 174
Wholesome Honey Sesame Cookies 175
Tangy Cranberry & Pistachio Cookies 176
Almond Marzipan Cookies 178
Salted Oatmeal Cookies 180
Pecan Cookies 181
Delicate Herb Cracker-Cookies 183
Freestyle Health Cookies 184

INDEX 187
CONVERSION CHARTS 190

INTRODUCTION

I am delighted to have this opportunity to write a new healthy baking book. The subjects of health and food have become closer to my heart in recent years, so I decided to investigate baking from a healthy perspective. Through conversations with my colleagues, I have discovered that the concept of what is "healthy" is definitely subject to perception. There are many different ways to understand this concept. Also, nutritional theories tend to change with time, as does what is considered "healthy".

This **Deliciously Healthy Baking** book is written from my own unique personal perspective. I believe that most of us want to eat in a healthy way and provide the right nutrients for our bodies. When it comes to baking, the issue of health becomes a bit more confusing and challenging than with regular cooking, especially when baking sweets. Indeed, for those of us who refuse to completely refrain from the enjoyment of eating pastries, this is not an easy issue.

The main approach to "healthy" in this book will therefore be the avoidance of the use of processed foods, by using high-quality, fresh ingredients instead. I also use whole-wheat flour extensively.

On those rare occasions when the recipe calls specifically for white flour, I use organic white flour instead of processed, bleached flour. In all recipes that require sweetening, I use cane sugar, brown sugar or honey; you can also replace these with agave nectar if it is available. Wherever applicable, I included a conversion key, so that you will able to choose what best suits you and your family.

This book was written after extensive research, including quite a few failures in my own home kitchen! I believe that this book reflects a unique outlook, rich and diverse, with a broad selection of healthy, delicious and energizing recipes for pastries, special breads, cakes and cookies.

You will surely discover a large selection of special recipes that you won't find in other books such as the Country Bread with Wakame Seaweed (page 126) and recipes that I developed during the work on this book. I have included the most delicious recipes, especially those that I prepare for friends, family and clients and that they request again and again.

This book is perfect for those who want to bake at home, insist on fresh home cooking and strive to provide their family with healthy products. The results will always be both tasty and healthy. It is important to note that there are no specific recommendations in this book for people with health problems. Those who watch their diet, however, will certainly be able to adapt some of these recipes with new ideas and options that fit their particular needs.

The book is designed both for hosting and everyday baking. Some of the recipes are easy to make and do not require special skills; some are slightly more complex in their preparation process, but definitely worth the effort!

It is important to read the recipes before you start. You will want to make sure that you have the necessary ingredients and that you understand the process. Most importantly. . . enjoy and Bon Appétit!

Avner Laskin

THE BAKER'S TOOLS

I always recommend using nonstick or silicone baking pans because they are easy to clean and require less greasing than other types of pans.

Recipes in this book call for the following baking pans:

— 12-cup muffin pans

— Baking pans
$10^1/_2$ x $15^1/_2$ x 1-inch jellyroll pan
9 x 13 x 2-inch baking pan

— Flat baking sheet
Can fit into your oven as well as your refrigerator

— Nonstick 5 x 10 x 3-inch loaf pan

— 8-inch Kugelhopf mold or small tube pan

Ovenproof ceramic cup or a heat-resistant container
To place inside the oven (This container generates extra steam throughout the baking process, which helps the dough to rise.)

Parchment paper
For lining pans and baking sheets (I recommend using sheets, since they are larger and do not curl like the rolls.)

Whisk
High-quality whisk for beating and emulsifying ingredients

Wide rubber or silicone spatula
For mixing and folding

Measuring cups & spoons
For accurate measurements

Long handle wooden spoon
For mixing

4-inch spatula
For general use

Stainless steel scraper
For dividing the dough

Plastic scraper
For dividing soft dough and scraping the sides of the bowls

12-inch palette knife
With a rounded top

10-inch Chef's knife (French knife)
With a broad, tapered shape and a fine edge

Good sharp knife
To make baker's signature marks on the top of breads

Serrated knife
For cutting baked products without ruining their texture
Note: Always keep kitchen knives sharp.

Pastry brush
Preferably with long soft bristles

20-inch pastry bag
Used for piping (I prefer this size of pastry bag because it holds a generous amount, is strong and doesn't leak. Use a silicone pastry bag, if possible, since it is easier to clean and does not absorb odors, colors or flavors.)

Pastry tips
Use a set of pastry tips that attach to your pastry bag securely.
Note: The recipes in this book call only for $1/_4$-inch pastry tip.

THE BAKER'S TOOLS

Wire cooling rack
For cooling hot baked goods once they are taken out of the oven (It allows the air to circulate evenly, preventing baked goods from getting soggy and moist while they are cooling.)

Rolling pin
There are various types of rolling pins used to roll out dough. Find the size and style that works best for you.

Set of bowls
Use an especially large, wide bowl to leave room for rising.

Kitchen towels
For baking bread, it is best to use 50% cotton and 50% linen.

Baking gloves
Use to protect your hands from hot pans.

Kitchen scale
Use a digital scale for accurate measurements.

Kitchen timer
Make sure you have an accurate timer.

Pizza stone
Buy a pizza stone that fits your oven. Slide it into the bottom of the oven or on the lowest rack. You can leave this stone on the floor of your oven all the time to soak up moisture, resulting in crispier baked goods. It also prevents burning. In order for it to work properly, it must be very hot. Be sure to place stone in cold oven before preheating.

Standing electric mixer
I recommend using a mixer with at least an 800-watt motor.

Be sure to use the right mixer attachment:

— **Wire whip**
   For whipping airy mixtures, such as egg whites

— **Dough hook**
   For mixing and kneading dough

— **Flat beater (paddle)**
   For mixing pastry dough while sweeping the sides of the bowl to incorporate all ingredients

Food processor with steel blade
For chopping, grinding or making a paste.

INGREDIENTS

One cannot bake without fat, sugars, etc. In this book, however, no artificial sweeteners, margarine or other substitutes are used. The healthy element in my baking comes from using fresh, organic products and real milk.

FLOURS

Bread flour

Bread flour does not undergo a bleaching process. It contains a higher percentage of protein than regular white flour. Using unbleached white flour adds strength and elasticity to the dough.

Whole rye flour

Use rye flour as a supplement to other types of flour. It is also a great base for sourdough preparation.

Whole-wheat flour

It is preferable to use stone-ground whole-wheat flour made from the entire wheat kernel, with nothing removed. This will give you the full benefits and nutrients of the wheat, directly from the fibers and the husk.

High gluten flour

High gluten flour gives the bread a chewy texture and works well with artisan breads made with whole-grain flours and sourdough. Be sure to always check the label on the package to ensure its protein content is about 14%.

Organic white flour

White, unbleached, all-purpose flour is used by itself or to blend with other flours for a finer-grain baked good.

INGREDIENTS

Note: Seeds and nuts should be stored in an airtight container in the freezer. Grind the seeds just before you use them. This will maintain their nutritional value. If you live in a warm climate, flours should also be refrigerated in an airtight container.

FIBER AND SEEDS

Wheat germ
Germ is essentially the part of a wheat plant that will later germinate and grow from the seed into the plant itself. Wheat germ is the most nutrient-rich portion of the wheat kernel.

Bran
This aids the digestion process.

Oats
All oats begin as groats—whole, unbroken grains. Before being processed into other forms of oats, groats are usually roasted at a very low temperature. This process gives oats their deep roasted flavor. The heat also activates enzymes that would otherwise cause the oats to decay, so the process extends their shelf life. Whole oat groats are becoming much easier to find these days. They're also processed into these common types of oats:

— **Steel-cut oats**
These are groats that have been sliced into two or three pieces. During baking, they retain their shape. Their flavor is nuttier than other types of oats. These shapely, steel-cut oats are becoming more readily available.

— **Rolled oats (old-fashioned oats)**
These are whole oat grains that have been steamed to make them soft and pliable, and then pressed under rollers and dried. The resulting "rolled oats" re-absorb water and cook quicker than whole groats or steel-cut oats. When a recipe calls for "rolled oats" it generally means the thickest type of rolled oat, which retains its shape during baking.

— **Oatmeal**
This consists of ground oat groats which are thinner than rolled oats. They add deeper flavor and texture to the bread and promote yeast activity.

Flax seeds
A wonderful taste enhancer with health benefits. Use freshly ground flax seeds for maxiumum nutritional value.

Fennel seeds
Add a dominant fullness and aroma to the flavor of any bread dough.

Poppy seeds
Use these seeds whole for breads. Make sure to grind them for making cakes.

Pumpkin seeds
Pumpkin seeds need to be lightly toasted before using them.
Toast them in either the oven or a toaster oven. They enhance the aroma of all baked goods.

Coriander seeds
These seeds add a strong flavor to your breads. Use only a pinch, as each little seed makes its presence felt with every bite!

Sunflower seeds
These are an excellent source of dietary fiber. They also add crispiness and a special taste.

INGREDIENTS

Sesame seeds

These add a nutty sesame flavor and a crunchy texture. Storing them in the freezer or refrigerator, in an airtight container, keeps them fresh. Lightly toasting them in a dry skillet right before baking brings out their flavor.

— **White sesame seeds**
These deepen the flavor of breads. Sesame seeds are very popular in Mediterranean countries. Unless stated otherwise, use raw white sesame seeds.

— **Brown sesame seeds**
These have a much more dominant taste than white sesame seeds, though still delicate. They are available at health food stores. If not avaliable, use toasted sesame seeds. Toasting enhances the sesame seed flavor.

— **Black sesame seeds**
These unique sesame seeds enrich the flavor of your breads with a special twist, making them more nutty and crunchy.

LIQUIDS AND OILS

Water
It is best to use cool mineral water, even in the winter, because the kneading process will warm the dough in any case.

Olive oil
Extra-virgin olive oil is my favorite. It has a deep flavor and adds a special golden tint to your breads.

Grape seed oil
Use grape seed oil when extra-virgin olive oil is not suitable. It has a high smoke point and leaves no aftertaste.

Milk
Adds a very unique color to recipes. It is best to use organic milk. Whenever possible, use an organic milk.

Eggs
Enrich the flavor and soften the bread. All of the recipes in this book call for large eggs.

Butter

Improves and deepens the flavor. I have yet to find a true supplement for real, pure butter. While it's true that excessive consumption is not good for your health, to butter's credit, fat increases the body's absorption of fat-soluble nutrients. For those who seek substitutes, the butter in a recipe can be replaced with clarified butter in a ratio of 1:1. Clarified butter is available at health food or Indian specialty stores, or you can even prepare it yourself. Whenever possible, use an organic butter.

Butter can be used in three ways: add melted butter at the start of kneading, add it at room temperature towards the end of kneading or fold it into the dough.

SWEETENERS

Agave nectar syrup

Naturally extracted from the agave plant, it is best known for its use in the making of tequila. It has a low glycemic index. Be sure to buy a product that is 100% agave without any additives. It is a delicious, high-quality substitute for white sugar. Although, it is 50% sweeter than sugar, it contains fewer calories per teaspoon. You can substitute it into recipes that call for honey as well.

Honey

I like the taste and color that it adds to the pastries. The flavor of honey will vary depending on the bees' diet. Honey has more calories per teaspoon than sugar, but has a sweeter taste.

Natural apple juice concentrate

This is the concentrated extraction of apples without added sugar. It has a high natural sugar content and tastes like real apples. It is not suitable for every recipe because of its distinct flavor. Two teaspoons of apple juice concentrate equal 1 teaspoon of sugar.

Unprocessed sugar

My guideline for this book was to avoid using processed foods as much as possible, so I did not use any artificial sweeteners.

A variety of sugars may be used in baking. Not only does sugar add sweetness, but it works in the baking process to add volume, texture, browning and as a perservative. Depending on the type of sugar used, these results may vary.

Cane sugar

It is produced from cane sugar syrup and has tiny, thin crystals. It is reasonably priced and readily available.

Molasses

This syrup is produced during the sugar refining process. It is rich in nutrition with lots of minerals, such as potassium, calcium, iron, vitamin B, niacin, choline and pantothenic acid. It usually has a strong aftertaste, which makes it a challenge to use. Molasses sugar without an aftertaste is very expensive and not readily available.

Muscovado sugar

This is a dark-colored sugar, since it is less refined and contains a large amount of molasses. It is moist and sticky with an aftertaste, so you should check to see if you like it before using it. Muscovado sugar is suitable for all baking, but note that it adds color to your final product.

Demerara

This semi-refined sugar is lighter than muscovado sugar. It is processed into large crystals that melt slowly. Demerara sugar is therefore suitable for sprinkling on pastries before baking.

INGREDIENTS

YEAST

There are two common types of yeast used in bread preparation: fresh and dry. In this book, most recipes call for active dry yeast, which is readily available. For different results, some recipes specifically call for fresh yeast.

Fresh yeast

This yeast is more delicate and slightly more aromatic. Its shelf life in the refrigerator is up to two weeks. Discard it when its corners have blackened and dried out.

For tender dough with high fat content, such as is used for brioches and krantz cake, I prefer to use fresh yeast.

If you need to convert dry yeast into fresh yeast, use the following conversion key:
Use 0.5 oz. of fresh yeast in place of 1 teaspoon of dry yeast.
Use 1 oz. of fresh yeast in place of 1^1/$_2$ teaspoons of dry yeast.
Use 2 oz. of fresh yeast in place of 1 tablespoon of dry yeast.

SOURDOUGH FOR BREADS AND YEAST DOUGH

Sourdough is a type of primitive yeast produced by the natural fermentation of starches and sugars. The pharaohs discovered sourdough in Egypt more than 3,000 years ago. In the baking community, sourdough is considered to be the elite and skilled bread to bake. Sourdough breads are the pride of any baker.

There are several ways to prepare sourdough, such as fermenting various fruits or sour milk. In this book, I chose two types of sourdough starter: a dark one that is based on rye flour, and a light version based on wheat flour.

It is very important to follow the explanations and instructions carefully without any deviation. Sourdough starter is very sensitive and unforgiving. Be sure to pay attention — if there is an error along the way, you will need to throw it out and start again.

DARK SOURDOUGH STARTER

STEP 1

$^1/_4$ cup rye flour
$^1/_4$ cup lukewarm water
1 tablespoon honey

1. Mix all the ingredients together in a bowl and cover with plastic wrap. Let it stand for 48 hours at room temperature.

2. After 48 hours, check to see if the mixture has fermented. (Bubbles on top indicate fermentation.)

3. If there are no bubbles, cover and let rest for 1 more day.

STEP 2

$^1/_2$ cup rye flour
$^1/_3$ cup water

Once the mixture from step 1 has fermented completely, mix in the rye flour and water. Cover with plastic wrap and let rest for 1 day.

STEP 3

1 cup rye flour
$^3/_4$ cup water

1. Check the dark sourdough starter, if it has tripled in size, the step was successful.

2. At this point, add the rye flour and water, mix well and cover with plastic wrap.

3. Let rest for 8 hours at room temperature.

STEP 4

2 cups rye flour
1 cup water

1. After 8 hours, transfer the mixture to the bowl of a standing electric mixer with a dough hook attached.

2. Add the rye flour and water and then knead on low speed for 5 minutes.

3. Transfer the resulting dough to a greased bowl, cover with plastic wrap and let rest for 6 hours.

4. Now the dark sourdough starter is ready for use in addition to, or instead of, yeast.

TO STORE AND USE DARK SOURDOUGH STARTER:

The dark sourdough starter can be stored in an airtight container or covered with plastic wrap in the refrigerator for up to 1 week. If more than a week passes, you will need to remove $^1/_2$ cup of the starter and replenish with rye flour and water using the following procedure, so it is active.

1. For each $^1/_2$ cup of sourdough starter that is used, stir in $^1/_4$ cup rye flour and $^1/_4$ cup water.

2. Let starter stand at room temperature overnight. Stir and return to refrigerator.

WHITE SOURDOUGH STARTER

PREPARATION TIME:
1 WEEK

STEP 1

¼ cup organic white flour
¼ cup lukewarm water
1 tablespoon honey

1. Mix all the ingredients together in a bowl and cover with plastic wrap. Let rest for 48 hours at room temperature.

2. After 48 hours, check to see if the mixture has fermented. (Bubbles on top indicate fermentation.)

3. If there are no bubbles, cover and let rest for 1 more day.

STEP 2

½ cup organic white flour
⅓ cup water

Once the mixture from step 1 has fermented completely, mix in the flour and water. Cover with plastic wrap and let rest for 1 day.

STEP 3

1 cup organic white flour
¾ cup water

1. Check the white sourdough starter, if it has tripled in size, the step was successful.

2. At this point, add the flour and the water, mix well and cover with plastic wrap.

3. Let rest for 8 hours at room temperature.

STEP 4

2 cups organic white flour
1 cup water

1. After 8 hours, transfer the mixture to the bowl of a standing electric mixer with a dough hook attached.

2. Add the flour and water and then knead on low speed for 5 minutes.

3. Transfer the resulting dough to a greased bowl, cover with plastic wrap and let rest for 6 hours.

4. Now the white sourdough starter is ready for use in addition to, or instead of, yeast.

TO STORE AND USE WHITE SOURDOUGH STARTER:

The white sourdough starter can be stored in an airtight container or covered with plastic wrap in the refrigerator for up to 1 week. If more than a week passes, you will need to remove ½ cup of the starter and replenish with organic white flour and water using the following procedure, so it is active.

1. For each ½ cup of sourdough starter that is used, stir in ¼ cup organic white flour and ¼ cup water.

2. Let starter stand at room temperature overnight. Stir and return to refrigerator.

THE BAKER'S TECHNIQUES

KNEADING

Combine liquids and yeast before adding the dry ingredients. This will dissolve the yeast and promote its activity.

Kneading bread and yeast dough refers to the action of combining all of the ingredients into the dough. For all the recipes in this book, use a standing electric mixer fitted with a dough hook. Knead each type of dough for exactly the time indicated in the recipe. A longer kneading time will result in a softer dough that is less firm.

The first 3 minutes of kneading are important for combining all the ingredients together. This step must be done at low speed.

Stopping the mixer between steps is necessary when adding nuts, dried fruit and chocolate. Be sure to keep the mixer running when the recipe calls for adding the salt 3 minutes into the kneading.

PROOFING

Applies to all dough that contains yeast.

First rising or resting time takes place just after finishing the kneading process. The purpose is to allow the yeast to start its action.

Final rising is the time during which the dough rises into its final shape.

Room temperature refers to 72°F. In warmer or colder places, you should try to place the dough in a place as close to this temperature as possible.

Before placing the dough in the oven the bread dough should rise to at least double its initial size, preferably a little more than double, but not triple.

Yeast cakes should triple their size by the end of rising time for a light and airy cake.

Do not let the dough over-rise. If the dough rises faster than the recipe directions indicate, proceed with baking and do not wait any additional time.

If the dough does not rise as quickly or does not double in size as directions indicate, it may be necessary to give the dough some more time.

If it has over-risen, it is possible that the dough will not succeed. Therefore, it is important to be attentive during rising time and to check its progress every 15 minutes.

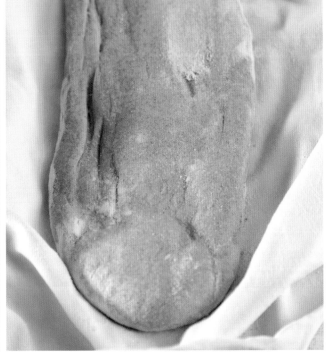

THE BAKER'S TECHNIQUES

BAKING TECHNIQUES

Electric ovens have two main heating options: one generated by the internal fan called convection, and the other by heating elements on the top and bottom of the oven.
Note: Be sure to preheat the oven before baking.

Convection ovens produce heat that is preferable when making pastries, cakes and cookies.

When baking bread use the heating elements without convection. This way, the heat slowly and thoroughly penetrates the dough from all directions and ensures maximum yeast or sourdough activity. The only drawback to this method is that the baking time is longer. The longer the bread is baked in the oven, the thicker and harder the crust will be. This method also ensures perfect baking from the inside.

Bake bread on a pizza stone, available at hardware, home or baking stores. The stone has a similar effect to a professional stove, dispersing the heat evenly to ensure better bread. Place on the bottom rack of the oven before preheating. Another option is to bake the bread in a loaf pan or on a baking sheet lined with a parchment paper.

To improve the bread's development during baking, I highly recommend pouring water in a ceramic cup or in a heat-resistant container and placing it inside the oven to generate steam throughout the baking process.

A gas oven, in which the heat rises from below, is very good for baking bread, but less recommended for baking yeast cakes and breakfast pastries. It is best to bake in a late model oven that has a number of baking modes.

Brushing tops of breads before baking by using liquids such as egg, olive oil or water results in a shinier and more pronounced bread color.

FULLY BAKED BREAD

To determine whether the bread is ready, remove the bread from the oven using a kitchen towel or baking gloves. Use the pad of your finger to knock the bottom of the bread. If you hear a hollow sound, the bread is ready. This test applies only to breads being baked directly on the stone.

For bread that is baked on a baking sheet, tap it on the side (not the bottom) and if you hear a hollow sound, the bread is ready. If your oven does not bake evenly, turn the bread after 15 minutes to ensure even baking.

THE BAKER'S TECHNIQUES

SHAPING

This is relevant only to the bread baking chapters and refers to shaping the dough into the desired shape. This step comes right after the dough has completed its first resting time.
In every recipe, I provide precise shaping instructions.

To roll a large piece of dough, hold one hand at a 45-degree angle and roll the dough backward and forward. Hold your other hand at the same angle, and simultaneously roll the dough up and down, while collecting the dough edges and pushing them underneath the ball.

To make an elongated loaf, first roll the dough into a ball. Then let it rest for five minutes on a floured work surface. Using both hands, roll the dough backwards and forwards until it forms an elongated shape.

For yeast bread recipes, the final shape can vary. Besides the classic elongated shape, it can be shaped however you like. Some possibilities are elliptical, "U", heart or square shapes. Use your imagination! However, for sourdough breads it is important to follow the recipe steps as instructed in order to achieve the best results.

A recipe for rolls can be used to make breads and vice versa.

THE BAKER'S MARK

This refers to those slashes that we see on a loaf of baked bread. There are two main reasons for these cuts:

First, the cuts allow the bread to reach its maximum rising potential.
The cuts on the top of the bread redirect the gas generated by the bread during the baking process. These gases have to be released through the cuts, instead of remaining inside to cause tearing or cracking of the bread in random places.

Second, the cuts are historic symbols and lend an aesthetic touch. Throughout the years, professional and artisan bakers make distinctive marks that distinguish their creations from others. Therefore, this term, translated from French, *La signature de boulanger,* is called the "baker's signature".

To make the slashes, use a sharp knife. It is important to decide ahead of time what shape cut you wish to make, and then slash the bread $1/8$-inch deep. Be sure to make a firm and decisive stroke. Otherwise, the blade will stick to the dough. This requires a bit of a practice, but practice makes perfect!

It is important not to make a slash by drawing the knife from one side of the dough to the other side in a single stroke. This will keep the ball of dough from becoming distorted. Therefore, cut 4 slashes instead of 2, even when making a cross-like shape.

BAKING TIPS

CAKE-MAKING TIPS

When mixing cakes be sure to add the ingredients to the mixing bowl slowly and gradually.

It is very important to grease the baking pan thoroughly to ensure that the cake will not stick during baking.

To test if a cake is ready, insert a toothpick in the center of cake. If the toothpick comes out clean, you're ready to go! If it doesn't, leave the cake in the oven for a few additional minutes. If necessary, turn the pan halfway through baking to ensure even browning.

Allow the cake to cool completely before slicing.

The best way to keep a cake fresh is to store it in an airtight container at room temperature for a few days.

COOKIE-MAKING TIPS

When preparing cookie dough it is very important to work the dough as little as possible. If overworked, the dough will begin to develop a 'gluten net' that is very difficult to work with. If this happens, let the dough rest for 45 minutes in the refrigerator and then continue with the process.

Before starting to prepare the cookie shapes be sure to have a baking sheet lined with a parchment paper ready. Additionally, make sure your oven is preheated and has reached the desired temperature.

When baking the cookies it is important to pay close attention during the baking process. Sometimes even a time difference of 1 minute can alter the final result.

When the cookies are ready allow them to cool completely before you pack them in an airtight container. Slightly warm cookies will sweat in the closed container and their texture will change from crunchy to soft.

HOMEMADE HEALTHY MORNING PASTRIES

IN THIS CHAPTER, YOU WILL FIND CLASSIC EUROPEAN PASTRIES ORIGINATING FROM FRANCE, ITALY AND SPAIN, BUT WITH A NEW AND EXCITING TWIST. FOR THOSE OF US WHO STRIVE TO MAINTAIN A HEALTHY DIET, THERE ARE TWO MAIN CHOICES: STOP EATING PASTRIES OR START BAKING IN A HEALTHIER WAY. THE IMPLICATION IS TO BE CONSCIOUS OF WHAT IS PUT INTO THE PASTRIES. USE LESS BUTTER THAN USUAL, WHOLE-WHEAT FLOUR, SUGAR CANE (VERY PALE BROWN), NATURAL SEEDS, ETC.

WITH THESE RECIPES YOU CAN ENJOY YOUR FAVORITE SWEETS WITH A LITTLE LESS GUILT.

RYE & OLIVE BREADSTICKS

MAKES 10 BREADSTICKS

Preparation time: 20 min.
Resting time: 70 min.
Rising time: 1¹/₂–2 hr.
Baking time: 20 min.

INGREDIENTS

1¹/₂ cups water

1 oz. fresh yeast or 1¹/₂ teaspoons
    active dry yeast

¹/₂ cup dark sourdough starter
    (see page 19)

1¹/₂ cups rye flour

2 cups whole-wheat flour

1 teaspoon salt

4 oz. black olives, pitted

1 tablespoon extra-virgin olive oil,
    for greasing the bowl

Additional flour for assorted tasks

These breadsticks are rich in flavor. They are perfect to serve as appetizers or as a morning pastry with a cup of fresh juice. Choose your favorite olives or use a combination of black and green olives.

PREPARATION

1. In the bowl of a standing electric mixer with the dough hook attached, mix the water, yeast, dark sourdough starter and flours at low speed for 3 minutes. With the machine running, add the salt, switch to medium speed and continue kneading for an additional 6 minutes.

2. Stop the machine. Add olives and knead at low speed for 1 minute, until evenly distributed.

3. Grease a medium bowl with the olive oil. Place the dough in the bowl, cover with plastic wrap and let rest until the dough has doubled in size. Check the dough after 1 hour.

4. Transfer the dough to a floured work surface. Using a dough scraper or sharp knife, divide the dough into 2 equal parts, then divide each part again into 5 pieces to make a total of 10.

5. Roll each piece into a ball and let rest for 10 minutes.

6. Place the palms of your hands on one ball and roll it backward and forward until it is 10 inches long. Repeat the process with the remaining pieces of dough.

7. Place the breadsticks ¹/₂-inch apart on a baking sheet lined with parchment paper. Let rise in a warm place until the dough has doubled in size, about 1¹/₂-2 hours.

8. Preheat the oven to 425°F 40 minutes before the end of the rising time. Once the breadsticks have risen, place them in the preheated oven. Then reduce heat to 400°F and bake for 20 minutes, or until golden brown.

9. Remove from oven. Allow to cool on a wire rack for 15 minutes before serving. Breadsticks stay fresh for a few hours. If they lose some of their crispiness, reheat them for a few minutes before serving.

MILK
& HONEY
MINI-ROLLS

MAKES 30 MINI-ROLLS

Preparation time: 20 min.
Resting time: 70 min.
Rising time: 1–1¹/₂ hr.
Baking time: 16 min.

INGREDIENTS

1¹/₂ cups whole milk
1 oz. fresh yeast or 1¹/₂ teaspoons
    active dry yeast
¹/₂ cup dark sourdough starter
    (see page 19)
2 tablespoons honey
1 cup rye flour
1¹/₂ cups whole-wheat flour
1 cup bread flour
2 teaspoons salt
1 tablespoon extra-virgin olive oil,
    for greasing the bowl
1 egg, beaten, for brushing

Garnish
1 tablespoon coarse sugar

Additional flour for assorted tasks

Special Tools
Ceramic cup or a heat-resistant
    container

PREPARATION

1. In the bowl of a standing electric mixer with the dough hook attached, mix the milk, yeast, dark sourdough starter, honey and flours at low speed for 3 minutes. With the machine running, add the salt, switch to medium speed and continue kneading for an additional 7 minutes.

2. Grease a medium bowl with the olive oil. Place the dough in the bowl, cover with plastic wrap or a large plastic bag and let rest until the dough has doubled in size. Check the dough after 1 hour.

3. Transfer the dough to a floured work surface Using a dough scraper or sharp knife, divide the dough into 5 equal parts, then divide each part into 6 pieces to make a total of 30.

4. Roll each piece into a ball and let rest on the floured work surface for 10 minutes.

5. Holding your hands at a 45-degree angle to the ball, use the outer edge of the palms to gently roll the dough backward and forward. Continue to roll until the dough is about 3 inches long and rounded in the center. Elongate and taper the ends of the balls into lemon shapes (see picture). Repeat the process with the remaining pieces of dough.

6. Arrange the rolls 1-inch apart on baking sheet lined with parchment paper. Using a sharp knife, make a slash, at a 45-degree angle, along the length of each roll. Brush with beaten egg and sprinkle with coarse sugar on top.

7. Let rise in a warm place until the dough has doubled in size, for about 1-1¹/₂ hours.

8. Preheat the oven to 425°F 40 minutes before the end of the rising time. Once the rolls have risen, place them in the preheated oven.

9. Pour water in a ceramic cup or in a heat-resistant container and place it inside the oven to generate steam throughout the baking process.

10. Reduce heat to 400°F and bake for 8-10 minutes, or until golden brown. Remove from oven. Allow to cool on a wire rack for 15 minutes before serving.

¤ *Milk & Honey Mini-Rolls*

SAVORY BREADSTICKS

Preparation time: 50 min.
Resting/Chilling time: 6^1/$_2$ hr.
Rising time: 1^1/$_2$–2 hr.
Baking time: 20–25 min.

INGREDIENTS

1^1/$_2$ cups whole milk

2 oz. fresh yeast or 1 tablespoon
  active dry yeast

2 tablespoons cane sugar or
  brown sugar

^{1}/$_4$ cup butter, room temperature

1 cup whole-wheat flour

1^1/$_2$ cups bread flour

1 cup whole rye flour

2 teaspoons salt

^{1}/$_2$ cup chilled butter, for folding

Garnish

^{1}/$_2$ cup oatmeal (see page 15)

^{1}/$_2$ cup cracked wheat

Additional flour for assorted tasks

PREPARATION

1. In the bowl of a standing electric mixer with the dough hook attached, mix the milk, yeast, sugar, butter and flours at low speed for 3 minutes. With the machine running, add the salt, then switch to medium speed and continue kneading for an additional 5 minutes.

2. Wrap the dough in several layers of plastic wrap. Let rest for 5 hours in the refrigerator.

3. Place the dough on a floured work surface and sprinkle a little flour on top. Using a lightly floured rolling pin, roll the dough into a 10 x 20-inch rectangle, ^{1}/$_2$-inch thick.

4. Between 2 pieces of parchment paper, roll out chilled butter into a 5x10-inch rectangle, about ^{1}/$_4$-inch thick. Chill butter 30 minutes. Remove the paper from the top of the butter and turn it over onto the dough. Remove the rest of the parchment paper and fold all four sides of the dough inward to cover the butter.

5. Sprinkle a little more flour on top of the dough and roll it out again to form the same size rectangle as before. Fold the long sides of the rectangle inward to form a 10 x 10-inch square; then fold it in half to form a 5 x 10-inch rectangle. Wrap the dough in plastic wrap and place in the refrigerator for 30 minutes.

6. Remove the dough from the refrigerator, place on a floured work surface and sprinkle a little flour on top. Once again, roll it into a 10 x 20-inch rectangle, $1/2$-inch thick. Fold the long sides of the rectangle inward and then fold the rectangle in half, just as before.

7. Wrap the dough in plastic wrap and place in the refrigerator for another 30 minutes. (At this point the dough can be frozen for up to 2 weeks. To use, thaw in refrigerator and proceed with the recipe.)

8. Prepare 2 separate small bowls: Fill one with water and the other with the oatmeal and cracked wheat (topping mixture). Using a wooden spoon or soft spatula, mix until the mixture is uniform.

9. Using a lightly floured rolling pin, roll the dough out on a floured surface to form a 9 x 20-inch rectangle. Cut the dough into strips, 9 inches long and $3/4$-inch wide.

10. Dip each strip in water, then roll in the topping mixture (prepared in Step 8), pressing gently so that the entire surface is evenly covered.

11. Arrange the slices $1/2$-inch apart on a baking sheet lined with parchment paper.

12. Let rise in a warm place until the dough has doubled in size, about $1^{1}/2$-2 hours.

13. Bake in a preheated 375°F oven for 20-25 minutes.

14. Remove from oven. Allow to cool on a wire rack for 20 minutes before serving. Breadsticks stay fresh for a few hours. If they lose some of their crispiness, reheat them for a few minutes before serving.

Cracked wheat, made from raw wheat kernels, is an excellent source of fiber. These savory breadsticks are perfect for breakfast and Sunday brunch.

LONG & TWISTED WHOLE-GRAIN BREADSTICKS

MAKES 24–26
BREADSTICKS

Preparation time: 50 min.
Resting/Chilling time: 6$^1/_2$ hr.
Rising time: 1$^1/_2$–2 hr.
Baking time: 20–25 min.

¤ *see photo on page 38*

INGREDIENTS

1$^1/_2$ cups whole milk
2 oz. fresh yeast or 1 tablespoon
    active dry yeast
2 teaspoons sugar
$^1/_4$ cup butter, room temperature
2 cups whole-wheat flour
1$^1/_2$ cups bread flour
2 teaspoons salt
$^1/_2$ cup chilled butter, for folding

Garnish
1 cup wheat bran
$^1/_2$ cup coarse bulgur wheat
1 teaspoon coarse salt

Additional flour for assorted tasks

PREPARATION

1. In the bowl of a standing electric mixer with the dough hook attached, mix the milk, yeast, sugar, butter and flours at low speed for 3 minutes. With the machine running, add the salt, switch to medium speed and continue kneading for an additional 5 minutes.

2. Wrap the dough in several layers of plastic wrap and let rest for 5 hours in the refrigerator.

3. Place the dough on a floured work surface and sprinkle a little flour on top. Using a lightly floured rolling pin, roll the dough into a 10 x 20-inch rectangle, $^1/_2$-inch thick.

4. Between 2 pieces of parchment paper, roll out chilled butter into a 5x10-inch rectangle, about $^1/_4$-inch thick. Chill butter 30 minutes. Remove the paper from the top of the butter and turn it over onto the dough. Remove the rest of the parchment paper and fold all four sides of the dough inward to cover the butter.

5. Sprinkle a little more flour on top of the dough and roll it out again to form the same size rectangle as before. Fold the long sides of the rectangle inward to form a 10 x 10-inch square; then fold it in half to form a 5 x 10-inch rectangle. Wrap the dough in plastic wrap and place in the refrigerator for 30 minutes.

6. Remove the dough from the refrigerator, place on a floured work surface and sprinkle a little flour on top. Once again, roll it into a 10 x 20-inch rectangle, $1/2$-inch thick. Fold the long sides of the rectangle inward and then fold the rectangle in half, just as before.

7. Wrap the dough in plastic wrap and place in the refrigerator for another 30 minutes. (At this point the dough can be frozen for up to 2 weeks. To use, thaw in refrigerator and proceed with the recipe.)

8. Prepare 2 separate medium bowls: Fill one with water and the other with bran and bulgur. Using a wooden spoon, mix until the mixture is uniform.

9. Using a lightly floured rolling pin, roll the dough on a floured surface to form a 9 x 20-inch rectangle. Cut the dough into strips, 9 inches long and $3/4$-inch wide.

10. Dip each strip in water, then roll in the topping mixture (prepared in Step 8), pressing gently so that the entire surface is evenly covered.

11. Hold the ends of each strip and gently twist the dough around itself by turning each hand in opposite directions. Repeat the process with the remaining pieces of dough.

12. Arrange the strips $1/2$-inch apart on a baking sheet lined with parchment paper.

13. Let rise in a warm place until the dough has doubled in size, about $1^1/2$-2 hours.

14. Bake in a preheated 375°F oven for 20-25 minutes.

15. Remove from oven. Allow to cool on a wire rack for 20 minutes before serving. Breadsticks stay fresh for a few hours. If they lose some of their crispiness, reheat them for a few minutes before serving.

These delightful breadsticks are twists full of crispiness, saltiness and a healthy coating of bulgur wheat and wheat bran. Both provide fiber, B vitamins and minerals for your diet.

¤ *Long & Twisted Whole-Grain Breadsticks (page 36)*

¤ Spiced Breadsticks with Poppy Seeds (page 40)

SPICED BREADSTICKS WITH POPPY SEEDS

MAKES 24–26
BREADSTICKS

Preparation time: 50 min.
Resting/Chilling time: 6^1/$_2$ hr.
Rising time: 1^1/$_2$–2 hr.
Baking time: 20–25 min.

¤ *see photo on page 39*

INGREDIENTS

1^1/$_4$ cups whole milk

1 egg

2 oz. fresh yeast or 1 tablespoon
   active dry yeast

2 teaspoons honey

^{1}/$_4$ cup butter, room temperature

2 cups whole-wheat flour

1^1/$_2$ cups bread flour

2 teaspoons salt

^{1}/$_2$ cup chilled butter, for folding

Garnish

^{2}/$_3$ cup whole poppy seeds

Additional flour for assorted tasks

PREPARATION

1. In the bowl of a standing electric mixer with the dough hook attached, mix the milk, egg, yeast, honey, butter and flours at low speed for 3 minutes. With the machine running, add the salt, switch to medium speed and continue kneading for an additional 5 minutes.

2. Wrap the dough in several layers of plastic wrap and let rest for 5 hours in the refrigerator.

3. Place the dough on a floured work surface and sprinkle a little flour on top. Using a lightly floured rolling pin, roll the dough into a 10 x 20-inch rectangle, ^{1}/$_2$- inch thick.

4. Between 2 pieces of parchment paper, roll out chilled butter into a 5x10-inch rectangle, about ^{1}/$_4$-inch thick. Chill butter 30 minutes. Remove the paper from the top of the butter and turn it over onto the dough. Remove the rest of the parchment paper and fold all four sides of the dough inward to cover the butter.

5. Sprinkle a little more flour on top of the dough and roll it out again to form the same size rectangle as before. Fold the long sides of the rectangle inward to form a 10 x 10-inch square; then fold it in half to form a 5 x 10-inch rectangle. Wrap the dough in plastic wrap and place in the refrigerator for 30 minutes.

6. Remove the dough from the refrigerator, place on a floured work surface and sprinkle a little flour on top. Once again, roll it into a 10 x 20-inch rectangle, $1/2$-inch thick. Fold the long sides of the rectangle inward and then fold the rectangle in half, just as before.

7. Wrap the dough in plastic wrap and place in the refrigerator for another 30 minutes. (At this point the dough can be frozen for up to 2 weeks. To use, thaw in refrigerator and proceed with the recipe.)

8. Prepare 2 separate medium bowls: Fill one with water and the other with poppy seeds.

9. Using a lightly floured rolling pin, roll the dough out on a floured surface to form a 9 x 20-inch rectangle. Cut the dough into strips, 9 inches long and $3/4$-inch wide.

10. Dip each strip in water, then roll in the poppy seeds, pressing gently so that the entire surface is evenly covered.

11. Hold the ends of each strip and gently twist the dough around itself by turning each hand in opposite directions. Repeat the process with the remaining pieces of dough.

12. Arrange the strips $1/2$-inch apart on a baking sheet lined with parchment paper.

13. Let rise in a warm place until the dough has doubled in size, about $1^1/2$-2 hours.

14. Bake in a preheated 375°F oven for 20-25 minutes.

15. Remove from oven. Allow to cool on a wire rack for 20 minutes before serving. Breadsticks stay fresh for a few hours. If they lose some of their crispiness, reheat them for a few minutes before serving.

I am a poppy seed enthusiast. Poppy seeds are the perfect ingredient for both breads and cakes. These spiced sticks are extra crunchy, which makes them a personal favorite.

CRUNCHY SESAME BAGELS

MAKES 12 BAGELS

Preparation time: 20 min.
Resting time: 70 min.
Rising time: 1¹/₂–2 hr.
Baking time: 18–20 min.

INGREDIENTS

¹/₂ cup whole milk

1 cup water

1 oz. fresh yeast or 1¹/₂ teaspoons
   active dry yeast

¹/₂ cup white sourdough starter
   (see page 20)

1 tablespoon extra-virgin olive oil,
   for dough

2¹/₂ cups whole-wheat flour

1 cup bread flour

2 teaspoons salt

1 tablespoon extra-virgin olive oil,
   for greasing the bowl

Garnish

1 cup raw sesame seeds

Additional flour for assorted tasks

PREPARATION

1. In the bowl of a standing electric mixer with the dough hook attached, mix the milk, water, yeast, white sourdough starter, olive oil and flours at low speed for 3 minutes. With the machine running, add the salt, switch to medium speed and continue kneading for an additional 7 minutes.

2. Grease a medium bowl with the second tablespoon of olive oil. Place the dough in the bowl, cover with plastic wrap or a large plastic bag, and let rest until dough has doubled in size. Check the dough after 1 hour.

3. Transfer the dough to a floured work surface. Using a dough scraper or a sharp knife, divide the dough into 2 equal parts, then divide each part into 6 pieces to make a total of 12. Roll each piece into a ball. Let rest on the floured work surface for 10 minutes.

4. Prepare 2 separate deep bowls: Fill one with cold water and the other with sesame seeds.

5. Roll each ball into a log about 10 inches long. Dip each log in water and then roll in the sesame seeds, pressing gently so that the entire surface is evenly covered. Form the logs into circles by overlapping the ends ¹/₂-inch. Press the ring closed. Repeat the process with the remaining pieces of dough.

6. Holding two sides of each circle, stretch slightly into an oval shape.

7. Place the bagels 1-inch apart on a baking sheet lined with parchment paper. Let rise in a warm place until the dough has doubled in size, about 1¹/₂-2 hours.

8. Preheat the oven to 425°F 40 minutes before the end of the rising time. Once the bagels have risen, place them in the preheated oven. Then reduce heat to 400°F and bake for 18-20 minutes, or until golden brown.

9. Remove from oven. Allow to cool on a wire rack for 15 minutes before serving.

BREADSTICKS WITH TOMATOES & HERBS

MAKES 24–26
BREADSTICKS

Preparation time: 50 min.
Resting/Chilling time: 6¹/₂ hr.
Rising time: 1¹/₂–2 hr.
Baking time: 20–25 min.

INGREDIENTS

¹/₂ pound whole peeled
  plum tomatoes, chopped
¹/₂ cup water
2 oz. fresh yeast or 1 tablespoon
  active dry yeast
12 fresh basil leaves
1 tablespoon fresh thyme leaves,
  coarsely chopped
1 cup parsley, coarsely chopped
¹/₄ cup butter, room temperature
2 cups whole-wheat flour
1¹/₂ cups bread flour
2 teaspoons salt
¹/₂ cup chilled butter, for folding
1 egg, beaten, for brushing

Additional flour for assorted tasks

PREPARATION

1. In the bowl of a standing electric mixer with the dough hook attached, mix the tomatoes, water, yeast, basil, thyme, chopped parsley, butter and flours at low speed for 3 minutes. With the machine running, add the salt, switch to medium speed and continue kneading for an additional 5 minutes.

2. Wrap the dough in several layers of plastic wrap. Let rest for 5 hours in the refrigerator.

3. Place the dough on a floured work surface and sprinkle a little flour on top. Using a lightly floured rolling pin, roll the dough into a 10 x 20-inch rectangle, ¹/₂-inch thick.

4. Between 2 pieces of parchment paper, roll out chilled butter into a 5x10-inch rectangle, about ¹/₄-inch thick. Chill butter 30 minutes. Remove the paper from the top of the butter and turn it over onto the dough. Remove the rest of the parchment paper and fold all four sides of the dough inward to cover the butter.

5. Sprinkle a little more flour on top of the dough and roll it out again to form the same size rectangle as before. Fold the long sides of the rectangle inward to form a 10 x 10-inch square; then fold it in half to form a 5 x 10-inch rectangle. Wrap the dough in plastic wrap and place in the refrigerator for 30 minutes.

6. Remove the dough from the refrigerator, place on a floured work surface and sprinkle a little flour on top. Once again, roll it into a 10 x 20-inch rectangle, $^1/_2$-inch thick. Fold the long sides of the rectangle inward and then fold the rectangle in half, just as before.

7. Wrap the dough in plastic wrap and place in the refrigerator for another 30 minutes. (At this point the dough can be frozen for up to 2 weeks. To use, thaw in refrigerator and proceed with the recipe.)

8. Using a lightly floured rolling pin, roll the dough out on a floured surface to form a 9 x 20-inch rectangle. Cut the dough into strips, 9 inches long and $^3/_4$-inch wide.

9. Arrange the slices $^1/_2$-inch apart on a baking sheet lined with parchment paper.

10. Let rise in a warm place until the dough has doubled in size, about $1^1/_2$-2 hours.

11. Brush with beaten egg and bake in a preheated 375°F oven for 20-25 minutes.

12. Remove from oven. Allow to cool on a wire rack for 20 minutes before serving. Breadsticks stay fresh for a few hours. If they lose some of their crispiness, reheat them for a few minutes before serving.

These aromatic breadsticks, an alternative to a sandwich, are the perfect way to start the morning, together with a cup of coffee and a glass of freshly squeezed orange juice.

SAVORY WHOLE-GRAIN PASTRY

Preparation time: 50 min.
Resting/Chilling time: 6¹/₂ hr.
Rising time: 1¹/₂–2 hr.
Baking time: 20–25 min.

INGREDIENTS

1¹/₄ cups whole milk

2 oz. fresh yeast or 1 tablespoon
   active dry yeast

2 teaspoons honey

¹/₄ cup butter, room temperature

2 cups whole-wheat flour

1¹/₂ cups bread flour

2 teaspoons salt

¹/₂ cup chilled butter, for folding

Grain Filling

¹/₂ cup oatmeal (see page 15)

¹/₄ cup raw sesame seeds

¹/₄ cup cracked wheat

¹/₄ cup butter, room temperature

1 teaspoon salt

Additional flour for assorted tasks

PREPARATION

1. In the bowl of a standing electric mixer with the dough hook attached, mix the milk, yeast, honey, butter and flours at low speed for 3 minutes. With the machine running, add the salt, switch to medium speed and continue kneading for an additional 5 minutes.

2. Wrap the dough in several layers of plastic wrap and let rest for 5 hours in the refrigerator.

3. Place the dough on a floured work surface and sprinkle a little flour on top. Using a lightly floured rolling pin, roll the dough into a 10 x 20-inch rectangle, ¹/₂-inch thick.

4. Between 2 pieces of parchment paper, roll out chilled butter into a 5x10-inch rectangle, about ¹/₄-inch thick. Chill butter 30 minutes. Remove the paper from the top of the butter and turn it over onto the dough. Remove the rest of the parchment paper and fold all four sides of the dough inward to cover the butter.

5. Sprinkle a little more flour on top of the dough and roll it out again to form the same size rectangle as before. Fold the long sides of the rectangle inward to form a 10 x 10-inch square; then fold it in half to form a 5 x 10-inch rectangle. Wrap the dough in plastic wrap and place in the refrigerator for 30 minutes.

6. Remove the dough from the refrigerator, place on a floured work surface and sprinkle a little flour on top. Once again, roll it into a 10 x 20-inch rectangle, $\frac{1}{2}$-inch thick. Fold the long sides of the rectangle inward and then fold the rectangle in half, just as before.

7. Wrap the dough in plastic wrap and place in the refrigerator for another 30 minutes. (At this point the dough can be frozen for up to 2 weeks. To use, thaw in refirgerator and proceed with the recipe.)

8. Meanwhile, prepare the filling: Place oatmeal, sesame seeds, cracked wheat, butter and salt in the bowl of a standing electric mixer. Beat with the mixer's flat beater on low speed until mixture is uniform.

9. Using a lightly floured rolling pin, roll the dough out on a floured surface to form a 5 x 25-inch rectangle.

10. Using a rubber spatula, spread the filling over the dough with rapid movements, evenly covering it.

11. Beginning at one long edge, roll the dough jellyroll style, ensuring that all the filling is inside.

12. Using a sharp knife, cut the roll into slices, $\frac{1}{2}$-inch thick. Place flat side down on a baking sheet lined with parchment paper, leaving 1 inch between slices.

13. Let rise in a warm place until the dough has doubled in size, about 1$\frac{1}{2}$-2 hours.

14. Bake in a preheated 375°F oven for 20-25 minutes, or until crispy.

15. Remove from oven. Allow to cool on a wire rack for 20 minutes before serving.

If you are looking for a pastry that will satisfy you throughout the morning until lunch, look no further — this whole-grain pastry is the ultimate pastry for you.

RYE BREADSTICKS WITH CHEESE

MAKES 10 BREADSTICKS

Preparation time: 20 min.
Resting time: 70 min.
Rising time: 1¹/₂–2 hr.
Baking time: 20 min.

INGREDIENTS

1¹/₂ cups water

1 oz. fresh yeast or 1¹/₂ teaspoons
   active dry yeast

¹/₂ cup white sourdough starter
   (see page 20)

1¹/₂ cups rye flour

2 cups whole-wheat flour

1 teaspoon salt

4 oz. Emmental cheese, shredded

1 tablespoon extra-virgin olive oil,
   for greasing the bowl

Additional flour for assorted tasks

This is a rich and filling pastry, perfect for guests or just simply to jump-start your morning. If Emmental cheese is not your favorite, replace it with any other Swiss or hard cheese that you prefer.

PREPARATION

1. In the bowl of a standing electric mixer with the dough hook attached, mix the water, yeast, white sourdough starter and flours at low speed for 3 minutes. With the machine running, add the salt, switch to medium speed and continue kneading for an additional 6 minutes.

2. Stop the machine. Add the cheese and knead at low speed for 1 minute, until incorporated.

3. Grease a medium bowl with the olive oil. Place the dough in the bowl, cover with plastic wrap or large plastic bag, and let rest until the dough has doubled in size. Check the dough after 1 hour.

4. Transfer the dough to a floured work surface. Using a dough scraper or sharp knife, divide the dough into 2 equal parts, then divide each part into 5 pieces to make a total of 10.

5. Roll each piece into a ball. Let rest on the floured work surface for 10 minutes.

6. Roll each ball into a log about 10 inches long. Place the breadsticks 1-inch apart on a baking sheet lined with parchment paper. Let rise in a warm place until the dough has doubled in size, about 1¹/₂-2 hours.

7. Preheat the oven to 425°F 40 minutes before the end of the rising time.

8. Once the breadsticks have risen, place them in the preheated oven. Then reduce heat to 400°F and bake for 20 minutes, or until golden brown.

9. Remove from oven. Allow to cool on a wire rack for 15 minutes before serving. Breadsticks stay fresh for a few hours. If they lose some of their crispiness, reheat them for a few minutes before serving.

SPECIAL WHOLE-GRAIN ROLLS

MAKES 12 ROLLS

Preparation time: 20 min.
Resting time: 1 hr.
Rising time: 1¹/₂–2 hr.
Baking time: 20–25 min.

INGREDIENTS

1¹/₄ cups rolled oats

¹/₄ cup whole sesame seeds

1 tablespoon flax seeds

1 tablespoon wheat bran

1³/₄ cups water

1 oz. fresh yeast or 1¹/₂ teaspoons
   active dry yeast

¹/₂ cup dark sourdough starter
   (see page 19)

1 cup rye flour

2 cups whole-wheat flour

2 teaspoons salt

1 tablespoon extra-virgin olive oil,
   for greasing the bowl

Additional flour for assorted tasks

Special Tools

Ceramic cup or a heat-resistant
   container

These rolls are perfect for making sandwiches at any time of the day. They have four grains, each offering your body exactly what it needs to run like a well-oiled machine!

PREPARATION

1. In a food processor fitted with metal blade or spice grinder, combine rolled oats, sesame seeds, flax seeds and bran, and grind until uniform.

2. In the bowl of a standing electric mixer with the dough hook attached, mix the water, yeast, dark sourdough starter, grain mixture (prepared in Step 1) and flours at low speed for 3 minutes. With the machine running, add the salt, switch to medium speed and knead for an additional 7 minutes.

3. Grease a medium bowl with the olive oil. Place the dough in the bowl, cover with plastic wrap or a large plastic bag and let rest until the dough has doubled in size. Check the dough after 1 hour.

4. Transfer the dough to a floured work surface. Using a dough scraper or sharp knife, divide the dough into 2 equal parts, then divide each into 6 pieces to make a total of 12.

5. Roll each piece into a ball and place the rolls ¹/₂-inch apart on a baking sheet lined with parchment paper.

6. Let rise in a warm place until the dough has doubled in size, about 1¹/₂-2 hours.

7. Preheat the oven to 425°F 40 minutes before the end of the rising time.

8. Once the rolls have risen, place them in the preheated oven.

9. Pour water in a ceramic cup or in a heat-resistant container and place it inside the oven to generate steam throughout the baking process.

10. Then reduce heat to 400°F and bake for 20-25 minutes, or until golden brown.

11. Remove from oven. Allow to cool on a wire rack for 15 minutes before serving.

CARAMEL-PECAN BUNS

Preparation time: 50 min.
Resting/Chilling time: 6$^1/_2$ hr.
Rising time: 1$^1/_2$–2 hr.
Baking time: 20–25 min.

INGREDIENTS

1$^1/_4$ cups whole milk

2 oz. fresh yeast or 1 tablespoon active dry yeast

3 tablespoons cane sugar or brown sugar

$^1/_4$ cup butter, room temperature

2 cups whole-wheat flour

1$^1/_2$ cups bread flour

2 teaspoons salt

$^1/_2$ cup chilled butter, for folding

Additional flour for assorted tasks

Caramel Sauce

$^3/_4$ cup molasses

2 tablespoons water

Pecan Filling

$^1/_2$ cup pecans, chopped

$^1/_2$ cup softened butter

$^1/_3$ cup powdered sugar

$^1/_2$ teaspoon ground cinnamon

Garnish

48 whole pecans

PREPARATION

1. In the bowl of a standing electric mixer with the dough hook attached, mix the milk, yeast, sugar, butter and flours at low speed for 3 minutes. With the machine running, add the salt, switch to medium speed and knead for an additional 5 minutes.

2. Wrap the dough in several layers of plastic wrap. Let rest for 5 hours in the refrigerator.

3. Place the dough on a floured work surface and sprinkle a little flour on top. Using a lightly floured rolling pin, roll the dough into a 10 x 20-inch rectangle, $^1/_2$-inch thick.

4. Between 2 pieces of parchment paper, roll out chilled butter into a 5x10-inch rectangle, about $^1/_4$-inch thick. Chill butter 30 minutes. Remove the paper from the top of the butter and turn it over onto the dough. Remove the rest of the parchment paper and fold all four sides of the dough inward to cover the butter.

5. Sprinkle a little more flour on top of the dough and roll it out again to form the same size rectangle as before. Fold the long sides of the rectangle inward to form a 10 x 10-inch square; then fold it in half to form a 5 x 10-inch rectangle. Wrap the dough in plastic wrap and place in the refrigerator for 30 minutes.

(continued on page 52)

¤ *Caramel-Pecan Buns*

(continued from page 50)

6. Prepare the caramel sauce: In a medium saucepan, heat the molasses and water over low heat, until the sugar dissolves and turns a dark caramel color.
Once the caramel is ready, quickly pour 2 teaspoons into each muffin cup.
If caramel begins to harden, return to the heat and stir until any hard caramel is melted. Set aside.

7. Meanwhile, prepare the pecan filling: Place the chopped pecans, ¹/₂ cup softened butter, powdered sugar and cinnamon in the bowl of a standing electric mixer.
Beat with the mixer's flat beater on low speed until mixture is uniform. Set aside for later use.

8. Remove the dough from the refrigerator, place on a floured work surface and sprinkle a little flour on top. Once again, roll it into a 10 x 20-inch rectangle, ¹/₂-inch thick. Fold the long sides of the rectangle inward and then fold the rectangle in half, just as before.

9. Wrap the dough in plastic wrap and place in the refrigerator for another 30 minutes. (At this point the dough can be frozen for up to 2 weeks. To use, thaw in refrigerator and proceed with the recipe.)

10. Using a lightly floured rolling pin, roll the dough out on a floured surface to form a 5 x 24-inch rectangle. Using a spatula, spread the filling evenly over the dough. Beginning at one long edge, roll the dough jellyroll style, ensuring that all the filling is inside.

11. Place 2 pecans inside each cup. Using a sharp knife, cut the roll into slices, each slice ¹/₂-inch thick. Place slices flat side down in each cup, on top of the pecans.

12. Let rise in a warm place until the dough has doubled in size, about 1¹/₂-2 hours. Bake in a preheated 375°F oven for 20-25 minutes or until golden brown.

13. Remove the muffin pan from the oven and carefully place the flat baking sheet on top of it (upside-down). Hold the two securely together and quickly flip the muffin pan over, so that the pastries fall onto the cold baking sheet. This needs to be done quickly while the pastries are still hot, so that the caramel will come out with the buns and not stay on the pan. Be sure to wear baking gloves.

14. Allow to cool on a wire rack for 30 minutes before serving.

Who does not love sticky buns? It is, of course, a great favorite with everyone. If you don't like pecans, you can replace them with any other kind of nut. The caramel enriches the pastry flavors and extends its freshness.

PISTACHIO & BROWN SUGAR FEAST

MAKES 14 PASTRIES

¤ see photo on page 54

Preparation time: 50 min.
Resting/Chilling time: 6^1/$_2$ hr.
Rising time: 1^1/$_2$–2 hr.
Baking time: 20–25 min.

INGREDIENTS

1^1/$_4$ cups whole milk
2 oz. fresh yeast or 1 tablespoon
　active dry yeast
3 tablespoons cane sugar or
　brown sugar
^{1}/$_4$ cup butter, room temperature
2 cups whole-wheat flour
1^1/$_2$ cups bread flour
2 teaspoons salt
^{1}/$_2$ cup chilled butter, for folding

Pistachio Filling
^{1}/$_2$ cup pistachios, finely ground
^{1}/$_2$ cup softened butter
^{1}/$_4$ cup almonds, finely ground
1 egg
3 tablespoons cane sugar or
　brown sugar
1 teaspoon brandy

Garnish
1 egg, beaten, for brushing
1 tablespoon cane sugar or
　brown sugar
2 tablespoons pistachios, finely ground

Additional flour for assorted tasks

PREPARATION

1. In the bowl of a standing electric mixer with the dough hook attached, mix the milk, yeast, sugar, butter and flours at low speed for 3 minutes. With the machine running, add the salt, switch to medium speed and knead for an additional 5 minutes.

2. Wrap the dough in several layers of plastic wrap. Let rest for 5 hours in the refrigerator. Place the dough on a floured work surface and sprinkle a little flour on top. Using a lightly floured rolling pin, roll the dough into a 10 x 20-inch rectangle, ^{1}/$_2$-inch thick.

3. Between 2 pieces of parchment paper, roll out chilled butter into a 5x10-inch rectangle, about ^{1}/$_4$-inch thick. Chill butter 30 minutes.

(continued on page 55)

(continued from page 53)

4. Remove the paper from the top of the butter and turn it over onto the dough. Remove the rest of the parchment paper and fold all four sides of the dough inward to cover the butter.

5. Sprinkle a little more flour on top of the dough and roll it out again to form the same size rectangle as before. Fold the long sides of the rectangle inward to form a 10 x 10-inch square; then fold it in half to form a 5 x 10-inch rectangle. Wrap the dough in plastic wrap and place in the refrigerator for 30 minutes.

6. Meanwhile, prepare the filling: Place ground pistachios, softened butter, ground almonds, egg, sugar and brandy in the bowl of a standing electric mixer. Beat with the mixer's flat beater on low speed until mixture is uniform. Set aside for later use.

7. Remove the dough from the refrigerator, place on a floured work surface and sprinkle a little flour on top. Once again, roll it into a 10 x 20-inch rectangle, $1/2$-inch thick. Fold the long sides of the rectangle inward and then fold the rectangle in half, just as before.

8. Wrap the dough in plastic wrap and place in the refrigerator for another 30 minutes. (At this point the dough can be frozen for up to 2 weeks. To use, thaw in refrigerator and proceed with the recipe.)

9. Using a lightly floured rolling pin, roll the dough out on a floured surface to form a 5 x 25-inch rectangle. Using a spatula, spread the filling evenly over the dough.

10. At bottom long edge, fold dough inward 2 inches. Repeat the process. Fold the top inwards about 1 inch to form a 2 x 25-inch rectangle, with a total of $2^{1}/_{2}$ folds. Press to flatten the roll slightly.

11. Using a sharp knife, cut the roll into slices, $1^{1}/_{2}$ inches wide. Place the slices $1/_{2}$-inch apart on a baking sheet lined with parchment paper.

12. Brush with beaten egg and sprinkle with sugar and ground pistachios on top. Let rise in a warm place until the dough has doubled in size, about $1^{1}/_{2}$-2 hours.

13. Bake in a preheated 375°F for 20-25 minutes, or until golden brown. Remove from oven. Allow to cool on a wire rack for 15 minutes before serving.

Pistachio is a very common ingredient in the Mediterranean basin, as well as in the patisserie shops of Paris. In this recipe I combine these two contrasting worlds, while still not forgetting the health factor.

DANISH-STYLE CHEESE POCKET & CHERRY PASTRY

MAKES 16 PASTRIES

Preparation time: 50 min.
Resting/Chilling time: 6¹/₂ hr.
Rising time: 1¹/₂–2 hr.
Baking time: 20–25 min.

INGREDIENTS

1¹/₄ cups whole milk

2 oz. fresh yeast or 1 tablespoon active dry yeast

3 tablespoons cane sugar or brown sugar

¹/₄ cup butter, room temperature

2 cups whole-wheat flour

1¹/₂ cups bread flour

2 teaspoons salt

¹/₂ cup chilled butter, for folding

Cheese Filling

1 cup part-skim ricotta cheese

1 egg

3 tablespoons honey

¹/₂ teaspoon vanilla extract

32 Amarena cherries (available at specialty baking stores)

1 egg, beaten, for brushing

Additional flour for assorted tasks

Special Tools

Pastry bag with ¹/₄-inch round tip

PREPARATION

1. In the bowl of a standing electric mixer with the dough hook attached, mix the milk, yeast, sugar, butter and flours at low speed for 3 minutes. With the machine running, add the salt, switch to medium speed and knead for an additional 5 minutes.

2. Wrap the dough in several layers of plastic wrap. Let rest for 5 hours in the refrigerator.

3. Place the dough on a floured work surface and sprinkle a little flour on top. Using a lightly floured rolling pin, roll the dough into a 10 x 20-inch rectangle, ¹/₂-inch thick.

4. Between 2 pieces of parchment paper, roll out chilled butter into a 5x10-inch rectangle, about ¹/₄-inch thick. Chill butter 30 minutes. Remove the paper from the top of the butter and turn it over onto the dough. Remove the rest of the parchment paper and fold all four sides of the dough inward to cover the butter.

5. Sprinkle a little more flour on top of the dough and roll it out again to form the same size rectangle as before. Fold the long sides of the rectangle inward to form a 10 x 10-inch square; then fold it in half to form a 5 x 10-inch rectangle. Wrap the dough in plastic wrap and place in the refrigerator for 30 minutes.

(continued on page 58)

¤ *Danish-Style Cheese Pocket & Cherry Pastry*

(continued from page 56)

6. Remove the dough from the refrigerator, place on a floured work surface and sprinkle a little flour on top. Once again, roll it into a 10 x 20-inch rectangle, $1/2$-inch thick. Fold the long sides of the rectangle inward and then fold the rectangle in half, just as before.

7. Wrap the dough in plastic wrap and place in the refrigerator for another 30 minutes.(At this point the dough can be frozen for up to 2 weeks. To use, thaw in refrigerator and proceed with the recipe.)

8. Meanwhile, prepare the filling: In a bowl, beat ricotta cheese, egg, honey and vanilla extract until mixture is smooth and uniform.

9. Using a lightly floured rolling pin, roll the dough out on a floured surface to form a 6 x 24-inch rectangle.

10. Using a sharp knife, cut the dough into 16 equal 3 x 3-inch squares.

11. Fill pastry bag with the filling and pipe 1 tablespoon onto the center of each square. Place one Amarena cherry on top of each.

12. Fold the top and bottom inwards over the filling to form flaps; then fold the sides inwards to create a mini-envelope and press the edges to seal it shut. Garnish with a cherry on the top of the folds (see picture). Repeat with the remaining pieces of dough.

13. Brush with beaten egg. Let rise in a warm place until the dough has doubled in size, about $1^{1}/_{2}$-2 hours.

14. Bake in a preheated 375°F oven for 20-25 minutes, or until golden brown.

15. Remove from oven. Allow to cool on a wire rack for 15 minutes before serving.

For all you cheese lovers out there, this is your pastry. You can lick your fingers and leave the guilt behind because I replaced the regular cream cheese with light Italian ricotta cheese, which is equally tasty and significantly lower in fat. In this recipe, you can exchange a teaspoon of fresh berries for each pastry in place of the cherries.

HEALTHY WHOLE-WHEAT CARROT PASTRY

MAKES 20 PASTRIES

Preparation time: 20 min.
Resting time: 1 hr.
Rising time: 1¹/₂–2 hr.
Baking time: 20 min.

INGREDIENTS

1¹/₂ cups whole milk

1 oz. fresh yeast or 1¹/₂ teaspoons
  active dry yeast

¹/₂ cup white sourdough starter
  (see page 20)

2 tablespoons honey

1 cup rye flour

1¹/₂ cups whole-wheat flour

1 cup bread flour

2 teaspoons salt

4 carrots, peeled and grated

5 tablespoons extra-virgin oil (for
  greasing the bowl and muffin pans)

Additional flour for assorted tasks

Special Tools
Two 12-cup muffin pans

From as early as I can remember, I have always associated carrots with good health. In fact, carrots provide our bodies with a range of essential nutrients.

PREPARATION

1. In the bowl of a standing electric mixer with the dough hook attached, mix the milk, yeast, white sourdough starter, honey and flours at low speed for 3 minutes. With the machine running, add the salt, switch to medium speed and knead for an additional 6 minutes.

2. Stop the machine. Add grated carrots and knead at low speed for 1 minute, until blended.

3. Grease a medium bowl with 1 tablespoon of the olive oil. Place the dough in the bowl, cover with plastic wrap or a large plastic bag and let rest until the dough has doubled in size. Check the dough after 1 hour.

4. Thoroughly grease each muffin pan with 2 tablespoons of olive oil.

5. Transfer the dough to a floured work surface. Using a dough scraper or sharp knife, divide the dough into 4 equal parts, then divide each part into 5 pieces to make a total of 20.

6. Roll each piece into a ball. Place a ball in each cup of muffin pan.

7. Let rise in a warm place until the dough has doubled in size, about 1¹/₂-2 hours.

8. Preheat the oven to 425°F 40 minutes before the end of the rising time.

9. Once the balls have risen, place them in the preheated oven. Then reduce heat to 400°F and bake for 20 minutes, or until golden brown.

10. Remove from oven. Allow to cool on a wire rack for 15 minutes before serving.

EXTRAORDINARY BREADS
FOR ORDINARY DAYS

NOTHING IS MORE ENTICING THAN THE SMELL OF FRESHLY BAKED BREAD COMING OUT OF THE OVEN — IT'S THE SMELL OF HOME. BAKING BREAD STEMS FROM LOVE: LOVE FOR THE PROCESS AND LOVE FOR THOSE WE ARE BAKING FOR. IN THIS CHAPTER YOU WILL FIND DAILY BREAD SELECTIONS TO MAKE FROM HIGH-QUALITY RAW INGREDIENTS. THESE BREADS REQUIRE A BIT OF TIME AND ATTENTION, BUT THEY ARE NOT COMPLEX.

BE SURE TO READ THE RECIPE IN ADVANCE, UNDERSTAND THE WHOLE PROCESS AND HAVE THE NECESSARY INGREDIENTS ON HAND. WITHIN A SHORT TIME, YOU WILL BECOME PROFICIENT. FROM THESE BREADS YOU CAN PREPARE SANDWICHES WITH VEGETABLES SUCH AS SPROUTS AND AVOCADO, TAHINI (SESAME PASTE) AND OTHER SUCH HEALTHY TREATS THAT YOU AND YOUR FAMILY LOVE! SERVE THE FRESH BREAD WITH SALADS OR PREPARE TOAST AND BRUSCHETTA USING YESTERDAY'S BREAD. YOU CAN EVEN CRUMBLE INTO BREADCRUMBS.

AROMATIC HERB BREAD

MAKES 1 LOAF

Preparation time: 30 min.
Resting time: 70 min.
Rising time: 1 hr.
Baking time: 32–37 min.

INGREDIENTS

1 cup water
1 oz. fresh yeast or 1 1/2 teaspoons
   active dry yeast
1/3 cup white sourdough starter
   (see page 20)
1/2 cup whole-wheat flour
2 cups bread flour
1 1/2 teaspoons salt
1 tablespoon parsley, coarsely chopped
1 tablespoon thyme, coarsely chopped
1 tablespoon oregano, coarsely chopped
1 tablespoon basil leaves,
   coarsely chopped
1 tablespoon extra-virgin olive oil

Additional flour for assorted tasks

Special Tools
Ceramic cup or a heat-resistant
   container

Herbs have a history of being used as remedies for physical ailments. Not only do herbs have potential for health benefits, but add unique flavor to foods.

PREPARATION

1. In the bowl of a standing electric mixer with the dough hook attached, mix the water, yeast, white sourdough starter and flours at low speed for 3 minutes. With the machine running, add the salt, chopped parsley, thyme, oregano, basil and olive oil, switch to medium speed and continue kneading for an additional 7 minutes.

2. Place the dough in a large greased bowl, cover with a kitchen towel and let rest at room temperature until the dough has doubled in size. Check the dough after 1 hour.

3. Transfer the dough to a floured work surface. Place the palms of both hands on the dough and roll it until it forms a ball. Let rest on the floured work surface for 10 minutes.

4. Place one ball on the work surface and use the palm of your hand to gently roll it backward and forward until it forms an elongated shape, 10 inches long, with slightly tapered ends.

5. Line a tray with a well-floured kitchen towel and place the dough on top. Let rise until the dough has doubled in size, about 1 hour.

6. Meanwhile, place a pizza stone on the bottom rack of the oven and preheat to 450°F. Carefully transfer dough to a floured pizza paddle. Using a sharp knife, make a slash, at an angle of 45 degrees, along the length of the bread.

7. Use pizza paddle to carefully place the dough on the stone. Pour water in a ceramic cup or a heat-resistant container and place in the oven to generate steam during baking.

8. Bake at 450°F for 7 minutes. Then reduce heat to 400°F and bake for an additional 25-30 minutes. The bread is ready when a knock on the bottom produces a hollow sound. Remove from oven. Allow to cool on a wire rack for 30 minutes before serving.

HEALTHY FOCACCIA

MAKES 1 LOAF

Preparation time: 30 min.
Resting time: 1 hr.
Rising time: 40 min.
Baking time: 32–35 min.

INGREDIENTS

1¼ cups water

1 oz. fresh yeast or 1½ teaspoons
   active dry yeast

⅓ cup white sourdough starter
   (see page 20)

1 cup whole-wheat flour

1½ cups bread flour

1½ teaspoons salt

4 tablespoons extra-virgin olive oil,
   for the dough

2 tablespoons extra-virgin olive oil,
   for greasing the bowl

Additional flour for assorted tasks

Garnish
¼ teaspoon coarse salt

Special Tools
10 x 15-inch (approximately)
   jellyroll pan
Ceramic cup or a heat-resistant
   container

PREPARATION

1. In the bowl of a standing electric mixer with the dough hook attached, mix the water, yeast, white sourdough starter and flours at low speed for 3 minutes. With the machine running, add the salt, switch to medium speed and continue kneading for an additional 2 minutes.

2. With the machine running, slowly drizzle 4 tablespoons of olive oil and continue kneading for 3 minutes until well blended.

3. Grease a large bowl with 2 tablespoons of olive oil. Place the dough in the bowl, cover with kitchen towel and let rest at room temperature until the dough has doubled in size. Check the dough after 1 hour.

4. Place dough in jellyroll pan. Lightly flour dough and gently flatten with your palm to fit into the pan. There is no need to be exact with this step.

5. Let rise in a warm place for 40 minutes.

6. Preheat oven to 450°F.

7. Use your fingers to make little indentations in the top of the dough. Drizzle the remaining 2 tablespoons of olive oil and sprinkle with salt.

8. Pour water in a ceramic cup or a heat-resistant container and place in the oven to generate steam during baking.

9. Bake at 450°F for 7 minutes. Then reduce heat to 400°F and bake for an additional 25-28 minutes. The bread is ready when a knock on the bottom produces a hollow sound.

10. Remove from oven. Allow to cool on a wire rack for 30 minutes before serving.

CLASSIC BRAIDED SHABBAT CHALLAH

MAKES 1 LOAF

Preparation time: 30 min.
Resting time: 70 min.
Rising time: 1 hr.
Baking time: 32–37 min.

INGREDIENTS

1¹/₄ cups water
1 oz. fresh yeast or 1¹/₂ teaspoons
   active dry yeast
¹/₃ cup white sourdough starter
   (see page 20)
2 tablespoons extra-virgin olive oil
2¹/₂ cups whole-wheat flour
1¹/₂ teaspoons salt

Additional flour for assorted tasks

Special Tools
Ceramic cup or a heat-resistant
   containe

PREPARATION

1. In the bowl of a standing electric mixer with the dough hook attached, mix the water, yeast, white sourdough starter, olive oil and flour at low speed for 3 minutes. With the machine running, add the salt, switch to medium speed and continue kneading for an additional 7 minutes.

2. Place the dough in a greased bowl, cover with a kitchen towel and let rest at room temperature, until the dough has doubled in size. Check the dough after 1 hour.

3. Transfer the dough to a floured work surface. Using a dough scraper or a knife, divide the dough into 3 equal pieces.

4. Roll each piece into a ball. Let rest on the floured work surface for 10 minutes.

5. Place the palms of the hands on one ball and roll it backward and forward until it is a rope, 12 inches long, with slightly tapered edges. Repeat with the other pieces of dough.

6. Place the three pieces next to each other. Fasten the top ends of the dough ropes together with a pinch. Pass the left-hand piece over the middle rope and then bring the right-hand piece over, repeating until there is no more dough left to braid. Pinch the ends together at the bottom.

7. Line a tray with a well-floured kitchen towel and place the raised braid on top. Let rise until the dough has doubled in size, about 1 hour.

8. Meanwhile, place a pizza stone on the bottom rack of the oven and preheat to 450°F. Carefully transfer dough to a floured pizza paddle. Use pizza paddle to carefully place the dough on the stone.

9. Pour water in a ceramic cup or a heat-resistant container and place in the oven to generate steam during baking.

10. Bake at 450°F for 7 minutes. Then reduce heat to 400°F and bake for an additional 25-30 minutes. The bread is ready when a knock on the bottom produces a hollow sound. Remove from oven. Allow to cool on a wire rack for 30 minutes before serving.

COUNTRY
RYE
BREAD

MAKES 1 LOAF

Preparation time: 30 min.
Resting time: 1 hr.
Rising time: 1 hr.
Baking time: 32–37 min.

INGREDIENTS

³/₄ cup water

1 oz. fresh yeast or 1¹/₂ teaspoons
   active dry yeast

²/₃ cup dark sourdough starter
   (see page 19)

¹/₂ cup spelt flour

2 cups whole rye flour

1 teaspoon salt

Additional flour for assorted tasks

Special Tools
Ceramic cup or a heat-resistant
   container

*This sourdough rye bread has a rich, country taste. In this recipe
I use spelt flour. It has a nuttier flavor and is rich with minerals.*

PREPARATION

1. In the bowl of a standing electric mixer with the dough hook attached, mix the water, yeast, dark sourdough starter and flours, at low speed for 3 minutes. With the machine running, add the salt, switch to medium speed and continue kneading for an additional 7 minutes.

2. Place the dough in a medium greased bowl, cover with a kitchen towel and let rest at room temperature, until the dough has doubled in size. Check the dough after 1 hour.

3. Transfer the dough to a floured work surface. Place the palms of both hands on the dough and roll it until it forms a ball.

4. Line a large bowl with a well-floured kitchen towel and place the dough inside.

5. Let rise until the dough has doubled in size, about 1 hour.

6. Meanwhile, place a pizza stone on the bottom rack of the oven and preheat to 450°F.

7. Carefully transfer the dough to a floured pizza paddle.

8. Use pizza paddle to carefully place the dough on the stone.

9. Pour water in a ceramic cup or a heat-resistant container and place in the oven to generate steam during baking.

10. Bake at 450°F for 7 minutes. Then reduce heat to 400°F and bake for an additional 25-30 minutes. The bread is ready when a knock on the bottom produces a hollow sound.

11. Remove from oven. Allow to cool on a wire rack for 30 minutes before serving.

WHOLE-WHEAT BREAD WITH FLAX SEEDS

MAKES 1 LOAF

Preparation time: 30 min.
Resting time: 1 hr.
Rising time: 1 hr.
Baking time: 32–37 min.

INGREDIENTS

³/₄ cup water

1 oz. fresh yeast or 1¹/₂ teaspoons
    active dry yeast

²/₃ cup dark sourdough starter
    (see page 19)

¹/₂ cup spelt flour

2 cups whole-wheat flour

1 teaspoon salt

2 tablespoons flax seeds, freshly
    ground

1 tablespoon extra-virgin olive oil

Additional flour for assorted tasks

Special Tools

Ceramic cup or a heat-resistant
    container

This bread is not only very tasty, but the flax seeds may provide health benefits for your body! It is best to buy whole flax seed and grind just before using.

PREPARATION

1. In the bowl of a standing electric mixer with the dough hook attached, mix the water, yeast, dark sourdough starter and flours at low speed for 3 minutes. With the machine running, add the salt, flax seeds and olive oil, switch to medium speed and continue kneading for an additional 7 minutes.

2. Place the dough in a greased bowl, cover with a kitchen towel and let rest at room temperature, until the dough has doubled in size. Check the dough after 1 hour.

3. Transfer the dough to a floured work surface. Place the palms of both hands on the dough and roll it until it forms a ball.

4. Line a large bowl with a well-floured kitchen towel and place the dough inside.

5. Let rise until the dough has doubled in size, about 1 hour.

6. Meanwhile, place a pizza stone on the bottom rack of the oven and preheat to 450°F.

7. Carefully transfer dough to a floured pizza paddle. Using a sharp knife, make 3 parallel slashes across the width of the bread.

8. Use pizza paddle to carefully place the dough on the stone.

9. Pour water in a ceramic cup or a heat-resistant container and place in the oven to generate steam during baking.

10. Bake at 450°F for 7 minutes. Then reduce heat to 400°F and bake for an additional 25-30 minutes. The bread is ready when a knock on the bottom produces a hollow sound.

11. Remove from oven. Allow to cool on a wire rack for 30 minutes before serving.

HEALTHY-HARVEST GRAIN BREAD

MAKES 1 LOAF

Preparation time: 30 min.
Resting time: 70 min.
Rising time: 1 hr.
Baking time: 37–40 min.

INGREDIENTS

1 tablespoon flax seeds

2 tablespoons raw sesame seeds

1 tablespoon poppy seeds

2 tablespoon rolled oats

1 cup water

1 oz. fresh yeast or 1¹/₂ teaspoons
   active dry yeast

¹/₃ cup white sourdough starter
   (see page 20)

¹/₂ cup spelt flour

2 cups whole-wheat flour

1¹/₂ teaspoons salt

Water, for brushing

Additional flour for assorted tasks

Special Tools
Ceramic cup or a heat-resistant
   container

PREPARATION

1. In a small bowl, mix together the flax, sesame and poppy seeds and rolled oats. Using a wooden spoon or spatula, stir until uniform. Set aside 1 tablespoon of the mixture for the grain topping.

2. In a food processor fitted with a metal blade or spice grinder, combine remainder of the grain mixture and process until coarsely ground.

3. In the bowl of a standing electric mixer with the dough hook attached, mix the water, yeast, white sourdough starter, flours and grain mixture (prepared in Step 2) at low speed for 3 minutes. With the machine running, add the salt, switch to medium speed and continue kneading for an additional 7 minutes.

4. Place the dough in a greased bowl, cover with a kitchen towel and let rest at room temperature, until the dough has doubled in size. Check the dough after 1 hour.

5. Transfer the dough to a floured work surface. Place the palms of both hands on the dough and roll it until it forms a ball. Let rest on the floured work surface for 10 minutes.

6. Place the ball on the work surface and use the palm of your hand to gently roll it backward and forward to form an elongated shape, 10 inches long, with slightly tapered ends.

(continued on page 74)

(continued from page 73)

7. Brush the top of the ball with water and sprinkle the remaining topping mixture (prepared in Step 1) on top.

8. Line a tray with a well-floured kitchen towel and place the dough on top, with the seed topping facing up. Let rise until the dough has doubled in size, about 1 hour.

9. Meanwhile, place a pizza stone on the bottom rack of the oven and preheat to 450°F.

10. Carefully transfer dough to a floured pizza paddle. Using a sharp knife, make a slash, at an angle of 45 degrees, along the length of the bread.

11. Use pizza paddle to carefully place the dough on the stone.

12. Pour water in a ceramic cup or a heat-resistant container and place in the oven to generate steam during baking.

13. Bake at 450°F for 7 minutes. Then reduce heat to 400°F and bake for an additional 30-33 minutes. The bread is ready when a knock on the bottom produces a hollow sound.

14. Remove from oven. Allow to cool on a wire rack for 30 minutes before serving.

This satisfying and hearty grain bread, rich in flavor, is excellent for sandwiches with avocado, greens, sprouts and tahini sauce.

TWO-COLOR HERB BREAD

MAKES 1 LOAF

Preparation time: 30 min.
Resting time: 70 min.
Rising time: 1 hr.
Baking time: 32–37 min.

INGREDIENTS

1 cup water

1 oz. fresh yeast or 1 1/2 teaspoons
  active dry yeast

1/3 cup dark sourdough starter
  (see page 19)

1/2 cup whole-wheat flour

2 cups bread flour

1 1/2 teaspoons salt

1 tablespoon parsley,
  coarsely chopped

1 tablespoon thyme, coarsely chopped

1 tablespoon oregano, coarsely
  chopped

1 tablespoon green basil leaves,
  coarsely chopped

3 tablespoons purple basil, finely
  chopped

2 teaspoons extra-virgin olive oil

Additional flour for assorted tasks

Special Tools

Ceramic cup or a heat-resistant
  container

PREPARATION

1. In the bowl of a standing electric mixer with the dough hook attached, mix the water, yeast, dark sourdough starter and flours at low speed for 3 minutes. With the machine running, add the salt, switch to medium speed and continue kneading for an additional 6 minutes.

2. Remove from bowl and divide the dough into 2 equal parts. Form 2 dough balls.

3. Place one ball into the mixer and add chopped parsley, thyme, oregano, green and purple chopped basil leaves and olive oil. Knead at low speed for 1 minute until well incorporated. Remove dough from bowl and set aside.

4. Place the two balls of dough in two separate greased bowls, cover with kitchen towels and let rest at room temperature, until the two doughs have doubled in size. Check the doughs after 1 hour.

5. Transfer the doughs to a floured work surface. Place the palms of both hands on one of the doughs and roll it until it forms a ball. Repeat with the other dough. Let rest on the floured work surface for 10 minutes.

6. Place the palms of the hands on one ball and roll it backward and forward until it is a rope, 15 inches long, with slightly tapered edges. Repeat the process with the other ball of dough.

(continued on page 76)

(continued from page 75)

7. Place the two pieces next to each other. Fasten the top ends of the dough ropes together with a pinch. Pass the left-hand piece over the right-hand piece and repeat until there is no more dough left. Pinch the ends together at the bottom.

8. Line a tray with a well-floured kitchen towel and place the dough on top. Let rise until the dough has doubled in size, about 1 hour.

9. Meanwhile, place a pizza stone on the bottom rack of the oven and preheat to 450°F.

10. Carefully transfer dough to a floured pizza paddle. Use pizza paddle to carefully place the dough on the stone.

11. Pour water in a ceramic cup or a heat-resistant container and place in the oven to generate steam during baking.

12. Bake at 450°F for 7 minutes. Then reduce heat to 400°F and bake for an additional 25-30 minutes. The bread is ready when a knock on the bottom produces a hollow sound.

13. Remove from oven. Allow to cool on a wire rack for 30 minutes before serving.

This bread is a playful mix of colors and flavors.

INDULGENT DARK CHOCOLATE SOURDOUGH BREAD

¤ see photo on page 79

MAKES 2 LOAVES

Preparation time: 30 min.
Resting time: 70 min.
Rising time: 1 hr.
Baking time: 27–30 min.

INGREDIENTS

1 cup water

1 oz. fresh yeast or $1^1/_2$ teaspoons active dry yeast

$^1/_2$ cup white sourdough starter (see page 20)

$^1/_4$ cup rye flour

$2^1/_4$ cups bread flour

$1^1/_2$ teaspoons salt

3 oz. dark chocolate, minimum 70% cocoa, coarsely chopped

Additional flour for assorted tasks

Special Tools

Ceramic cup or a heat-resistant container

PREPARATION

1. In the bowl of a standing electric mixer with the dough hook attached, mix the water, yeast, white sourdough starter and flours at low speed for 3 minutes. With the machine running, add the salt, switch to medium speed and continue kneading for an additional 6 minutes.

2. Stop the machine. Add chopped chocolate and knead at low speed for 1 minute, until well blended.

3. Place the dough in a greased bowl, cover with a kitchen towel and let rest at room temperature, until the dough has doubled in size. Check the dough after 1 hour.

4. Transfer the dough to a floured work surface. Divide into two equal pieces. Place the palms of both hands on one piece of the dough and roll it until it forms a ball. Repeat with remaining dough. Let rest on the floured work surface for 10 minutes.

5. Place one ball on the work surface and use the palms of the hands to gently roll ball of dough backward and forward until it forms an elongated shape, 10 inches long, with tapered ends. Repeat with remaining ball of dough.

(continued on page 78)

(continued from page 77)

6. Line a tray with a well-floured kitchen towel and place the dough on top. Let rise until the loaves have doubled in size, about 1 hour.

7. Meanwhile, place a pizza stone on the bottom rack of the oven and preheat to 450°F.

8. Carefully transfer dough to a floured pizza paddle. Using a sharp knife, make a slash, at an angle of 45 degrees, along the length of the bread.

9. Use pizza paddle to carefully place the dough on the stone.

10. Pour water in a ceramic cup or a heat-resistant container and place in the oven to generate steam during baking.

11. Bake at 450°F for 7 minutes. Then reduce heat to 400°F and bake for an additional 20-23 minutes. The bread is ready when a knock on the bottom produces a hollow sound.

12. Remove from oven. Allow to cool on a wire rack for 30 minutes before serving.

This bread has the most surprising taste — take one bite and you will immediately understand why it's unique!

¤ *Indulgent Dark Chocolate Sourdough Bread*

¤ *Worker's Dark Bread*

WORKER'S DARK BREAD

MAKES 1 LOAF

Preparation time: 30 min.
Resting time: 70 min.
Rising time: 1 hr.
Baking time: 32–37 min.

INGREDIENTS

1 cup water
1 oz. fresh yeast or 1$^1/_2$ teaspoons
    active dry yeast
$^1/_2$ cup dark sourdough starter
    (see page 19)
$^1/_2$ cup whole-wheat flour
2 cups bread flour
1$^1/_2$ teaspoons salt

Additional flour for assorted tasks

Special Tools
Ceramic cup or a heat-resistant
    container

PREPARATION

1. In the bowl of a standing electric mixer with the dough hook attached, mix the water, yeast, dark sourdough starter and flours at low speed for 3 minutes. With the machine running, add the salt, switch to medium speed and continue kneading for an additional 7 minutes.

2. Place the dough in a large greased bowl, cover with a kitchen towel and let rest at room temperature until the dough has doubled in size. Check the dough after 1 hour.

3. Transfer the dough to a floured work surface. Place the palms of both hands on the dough and roll it until it forms a ball. Let rest on the floured work surface for 10 minutes.

4. Place ball on the work surface and use the palms of the hands to gently roll it backward and forward until it forms an elongated shape, 10 inches long, with slightly tapered ends.

5. Line a tray with a well-floured kitchen towel and place the dough on top. Let rise until the dough has doubled in size, about 1 hour.

6. Meanwhile, place a pizza stone on the bottom rack of the oven and preheat to 450°F.

7. Carefully transfer dough to a floured pizza paddle. Using a sharp knife, make 3 slashes, at a 45-degree angle, across the width of the bread.

8. Use pizza paddle to carefully place the dough on the stone.

9. Pour water in a ceramic cup or a heat-resistant container and place in the oven to generate steam during baking.

10. Bake at 450°F for 7 minutes. Then reduce heat to 400°F and bake for an additional 25-30 minutes. The bread is ready when a knock on the bottom produces a hollow sound.

11. Remove from oven. Allow to cool on a wire rack for 30 minutes before serving.

FRENCH-STYLE COUNTRY BREAD

MAKES 1 LOAF

Preparation time: 30 min.
Resting time: 1 hr.
Rising time: 1 hr.
Baking time: 32–37 min.

INGREDIENTS

³/₄ cup water

1 oz. fresh yeast or 1¹/₂ teaspoons active dry yeast

¹/₂ cup white sourdough starter (see page 20)

¹/₂ cup whole-wheat flour

¹/₄ cup rye flour

2 cups bread flour

1 teaspoon salt

Additional flour for assorted tasks

Special Tools
Ceramic cup or a heat-resistant container

This bread has the classic French taste. Eaten fresh it is obviously a delight and you can use it to prepare toast or bruschetta two or three days after baking.

PREPARATION

1. In the bowl of a standing electric mixer with the dough hook attached, mix the water, yeast, white sourdough starter and flours at low speed for 3 minutes. With the machine running, add the salt, switch to medium speed and continue kneading for an additional 7 minutes.

2. Place the dough in a greased bowl, cover with a kitchen towel and let rest at room temperature until the dough has doubled in size. Check the dough after 1 hour.

3. Transfer the dough to a floured work surface. Place the palms of both hands on the dough and roll it until it forms a ball.

4. Line a large bowl with a well-floured kitchen towel and place the dough inside. Let rise until the dough has doubled in size, about 1 hour.

5. Meanwhile, place a pizza stone on the bottom rack of the oven and preheat to 450°F.

6. Carefully transfer dough to a floured pizza paddle. Using a sharp knife, make 2 parallel slashes across the width of the bread. Turn the dough 90 degrees and repeat the process.

7. Use pizza paddle to carefully place the dough on the stone.

8. Pour water in a ceramic cup or a heat-resistant container and place in the oven to generate steam during baking.

9. Bake at 450°F for 7 minutes. Then reduce heat to 400°F and bake for an additional 25-30 minutes. The bread is ready when a knock on the bottom produces a hollow sound.

10. Remove from oven. Allow to cool on a wire rack for 30 minutes before serving.

¤ *French-Style Country Bread*

PARMESAN ROLLS

MAKES 12 ROLLS

Preparation time: 20 min.
Resting time: 70 min.
Rising time: 1 hr.
Baking time: 15–20 min.

INGREDIENTS

$1^1/_2$ cups water

1 oz. fresh yeast or $1^1/_2$ teaspoons
   active dry yeast

$1/_2$ cup white sourdough starter
   (see page 20)

2 tablespoons extra-virgin olive oil,
   for dough

$1/_2$ cup whole-wheat flour

3 cups bread flour

2 teaspoons salt

$1/_2$ cup Parmesan cheese, grated

1 tablespoon extra-virgin olive oil,
   for greasing the bowl

Additional flour for assorted tasks

Special Tools
Ceramic cup or a heat-resistant
   container

My family just can't get enough of these rolls! They are a great alternative to traditional dinner rolls and fancy enough for a gourmet dinner party.

PREPARATION

1. In the bowl of a standing electric mixer with the dough hook attached, mix the water, yeast, white sourdough starter, olive oil and flours at low speed for 3 minutes. With the machine running, add the salt, switch to medium speed and continue kneading for an additional 5 minutes.

2. Stop the machine. Add Parmesan cheese and knead at low speed for 2 minutes, until evenly distributed.

3. Grease a medium bowl with 1 tablespoon of olive oil. Place the dough in greased bowl, cover with plastic wrap or a large plastic bag and let rest until the dough has doubled in size. Check the dough after 1 hour.

4. Transfer the dough to a floured work surface. Divide the dough into 2 equal parts, then divide each part into 6 pieces to make a total of 12. Roll each piece into a ball. Let rest on the floured work surface for 10 minutes.

5. Place the rolls 1-inch apart on a baking sheet lined with parchment paper. Let rise in a warm place until the dough has doubled in size, about 1 hour.

6. Preheat the oven to 425°F 30 minutes before the end of the rising time.

7. Pour water in a ceramic cup or in a heat-resistant container and place it inside the oven to generate steam throughout the baking process.

8. Once the rolls have risen, place them in the preheated oven. Then reduce heat to 400°F and bake for 15-20 minutes, or until golden brown.

9. Remove from oven. Allow to cool on a wire rack for 15 minutes before serving.

HEARTY RYE BREAD WITH DRIED FRUIT

MAKES 1 LOAF

Preparation time: 30 min.
Resting time: 1 hr.
Rising time: 1 hr.
Baking time: 32–37 min.

INGREDIENTS

3/4 cup water

1 oz. fresh yeast or 1 1/2 teaspoons
   active dry yeast

2/3 cup dark sourdough starter
   (see page 19)

1/2 cup spelt flour

2 cups whole rye flour

1 teaspoon salt

2 tablespoons raisins

2 tablespoons golden raisins

2 tablespoons dried cranberries

1 tablespoon dried blueberries

Additional flour for assorted tasks

Special Tools
Ceramic cup or a heat-resistant
   container

Blueberries and cranberries are powerful antioxidants. You can reap their benefits in this delicious bread. I like to use it to make sandwiches with tangy gorgonzola cheese.

PREPARATION

1. In the bowl of a standing electric mixer with the dough hook attached, mix the water, yeast, dark sourdough starter and flours at low speed for 3 minutes. With the machine running, add the salt, switch to medium speed and continue kneading for an additional 6 minutes.

2. Stop the machine. Add raisins, cranberries and blueberries and knead at low speed for 2 minutes, until evenly distributed.

3. Place the dough in a greased bowl, cover with a kitchen towel and let rest at room temperature until the dough has doubled in size. Check the dough after 1 hour.

4. Transfer the dough to a floured work surface. Place the palms of both hands on the dough and roll it until it forms a ball.

5. Line a large bowl with a well-floured kitchen towel and place the dough inside. Let rise until the dough has doubled in size, about 1 hour.

6. Meanwhile, place a pizza stone on the bottom rack of the oven and preheat to 450°F.

7. Carefully transfer dough to a floured pizza paddle so that the top is now facing downward. Use pizza paddle to carefully place the dough on the stone.

8. Pour water in a ceramic cup or a heat-resistant container and place in the oven to generate steam during baking.

9. Bake at 450°F for 7 minutes. Then reduce heat to 400°F and bake for an additional 25-30 minutes. The bread is ready when a knock on the bottom produces a hollow sound.

10. Remove from oven. Allow to cool on a wire rack for 30 minutes before serving.

DARK CLASSIC COUNTRY BAGUETTES

MAKES 3 BAGUETTES

Preparation time: 30 min.
Resting time: 1¼ hr.
Rising time: 1 hr.
Baking time: 22–25 min.

INGREDIENTS

1 cup water
1 oz. fresh yeast or 1½ teaspoons
   active dry yeast
½ cup dark sourdough starter
   (see page 19)
1 cup whole-wheat flour
1½ cups bread flour
1½ teaspoons salt

Additional flour for assorted tasks

Special Tools
Ceramic cup or a heat-resistant
   container

PREPARATION

1. In the bowl of a standing electric mixer with the dough hook attached, mix the water, yeast, dark sourdough starter and flours at low speed for 3 minutes. With the machine running, add the salt, switch to medium speed and continue kneading for an additional 7 minutes.

2. Place the dough in a greased bowl, cover with a kitchen towel and let rest at room temperature until the dough has doubled in size. Check the dough after 1 hour.

3. Transfer the dough to a floured work surface. Divide the dough into 3 equal pieces and roll each piece into a ball. Let rest on the floured work surface for 10 minutes.

4. Place the palms of the hands on one ball and roll it backward and forward until it forms an elongated shape, 10 inches long. Repeat with other dough pieces. Let rest for 5 minutes.

5. Roll one piece of dough until it reaches a 20-inch long baguette shape with slightly tapered ends. Repeat with the other dough pieces.

6. Line a tray with a well-floured kitchen towel and place the baguettes on top. Let rise until the dough has doubled in size, about 1 hour.

7. Meanwhile, place a pizza stone on the bottom rack of the oven and preheat to 450°F.

8. Carefully transfer dough to a floured pizza paddle. Using a sharp knife, make 5 slashes, at a 45-degree angle, along the length of each baguette.

9. Use pizza paddle to carefully place each baguette on the stone. Pour water in a ceramic cup or a heat-resistant container and place in the oven to generate steam during baking.

10. Bake at 450°F for 7 minutes. Then reduce heat to 400°F and bake for an additional 15-18 minutes. The bread is ready when a knock on the bottom produces a hollow sound.

11. Remove from oven. Allow to cool on a wire rack for 30 minutes before serving.

¤ *Dark Classic Country Baguettes*

MEDITERRANEAN SESAME-COATED BREAD

MAKES 2 LOAVES

Preparation time: 30 min.
Resting time: 70 min.
Rising time: 1 hr.
Baking time: 32–37 min.

INGREDIENTS

1¹/₄ cups water

1 oz. fresh yeast or 1¹/₂ teaspoons
   active dry yeast

¹/₂ cup white sourdough starter
   (see page 20)

¹/₄ cup raw sesame seeds

1 cup whole-wheat flour

1¹/₂ cups bread flour

1¹/₂ teaspoons salt

Water, for brushing

Garnish

2 tablespoons raw sesame seeds

Additional flour for assorted tasks

Special Tools

Ceramic cup or a heat-resistant
   container

PREPARATION

1. In the bowl of a standing electric mixer with the dough hook attached, mix the water, yeast, white sourdough starter, sesame seeds and flours at low speed for 3 minutes. With the machine running, add the salt, switch to medium speed and continue kneading for an additional 7 minutes.

2. Place the dough in a greased bowl, cover with a kitchen towel and let rest at room temperature, until the dough has doubled in size. Check the dough after 1 hour.

3. Transfer the dough to a floured work surface. Divide the dough into 2 equal pieces and roll each piece into a ball. Let rest on the floured work surface for 10 minutes.

4. Place your palms on one ball and roll it backward and forward until it is an elongated shape, 10 inches long. Repeat with the other ball of dough.

5. Brush the top of the loaves with water and sprinkle the sesame seeds on top to garnish.

6. Line a tray with a well-floured kitchen towel and place the loaves on top.

7. Let rise about until the dough has doubled in size, about 1 hour.

8. Meanwhile, place a pizza stone on the bottom rack of the oven and preheat to 450°F.

9. Carefully transfer dough to a floured pizza paddle. Using a sharp knife, make 3 slashes, at an angle of 45 degrees, along the length of each loaf.

10. Use pizza paddle to carefully place each loaf on the stone.

11. Pour water in a ceramic cup or a heat-resistant container and place in the oven to generate steam during baking.

12. Bake at 450°F for 7 minutes. Then reduce heat to 400°F and bake for an additional 25-30 minutes. The bread is ready when a knock on the bottom produces a hollow sound.

13. Remove from oven. Allow to cool on a wire rack for 30 minutes before serving.

This bread has a thick, crispy outer crust. The sesame seed gives a wonderful aroma and lip-smacking taste. This is my favorite bread to wipe my plate clean after a good meal.

CLASSIC
RYE
BAGELS

MAKES 12 BAGELS

Preparation time: 20 min.
Resting time: 70 min.
Rising time: 1¹/₂–2 hr.
Baking time: 18–20 min.

INGREDIENTS

1¹/₂ cups water

1 oz. fresh yeast or 1¹/₂ teaspoons
  active dry yeast

1 teaspoon honey

¹/₂ cup dark sourdough starter
  (see page 19)

1 tablespoon extra-virgin olive oil,
  for dough

1 cup whole rye flour

2¹/₂ cups bread flour

2 teaspoons salt

1 tablespoon extra-virgin olive oil,
  for greasing the bowl

Garnish

¹/₂ cup wheat bran

Additional flour for assorted tasks

PREPARATION

1. In the bowl of a standing electric mixer with the dough hook attached, mix the water, yeast, honey, dark sourdough starter, olive oil and flours at low speed for 3 minutes. With the machine running, add the salt, switch to medium speed and continue kneading for an additional 7 minutes.

2. Grease a medium bowl with 1 tablespoon of olive oil. Place the dough in the bowl, cover with plastic wrap or a large plastic bag and let rest until the dough has doubled in size. Check the dough after 1 hour.

3. Transfer the dough to a floured work surface. Using a dough scraper or a knife, divide the dough into 2 equal parts, then divide each part into 6 pieces to make a total of 12. Roll each piece into a ball. Let rest on the floured work surface for 10 minutes.

4. Prepare 2 separate deep bowls: Fill one with cold water and the other with bran.

5. Roll each ball into a log about 10 inches long. Dip each log in water and then roll in the sesame seeds, pressing gently so that the entire surface is evenly covered. Form the logs into circles by overlapping the ends ¹/₂-inch. Press the ring closed. Repeat the process with the remaining pieces of dough.

6. Holding two sides of each circle, stretch slightly into an oval shape.

7. Place the bagels 1-inch apart on a baking sheet lined with parchment paper.

8. Let rise in a warm place until the dough has doubled in size, about 1¹/₂-2 hours.

9. Preheat the oven to 425°F 40 minutes before the end of the rising time.

10. Once the bagels have risen, place them in the preheated oven. Then reduce heat to 400°F and bake the rolls for 18-20 minutes, or until golden brown and crispy.

11. Remove from oven. Allow to cool on a wire rack for 15 minutes before serving.

¤ *Beet & Anise Bread*

BEET & ANISE BREAD

MAKES 2 LOAVES

Preparation time: 30 min.
Resting time: 70 min.
Rising time: 1 hr.
Baking time: 32–37 min.

INGREDIENTS

1¹/₂ cups water
1 fresh beet, peeled and sliced
1 tablespoon extra-virgin oil
1 oz. fresh yeast or 1¹/₂ teaspoons
   active dry yeast
¹/₂ cup white sourdough starter
   (see page 20)
1 tablespoon anise seeds
1 cup whole-wheat flour
1¹/₂ cups bread flour
1¹/₂ teaspoons salt

Additional flour for assorted tasks

Special Tools
Ceramic cup or a heat-resistant
   container

PREPARATION

1. In a food processor fitted with a metal blade or a blender, combine the water, sliced beet and olive oil. Process until a smooth paste is achieved.

2. In the bowl of a standing electric mixer with the dough hook attached, mix the beet paste, yeast, white sourdough starter, anise seeds and flours at low speed for 3 minutes. With the machine running, add the salt, switch to medium speed and continue kneading for an additional 7 minutes.

3. Place the dough in a greased bowl, cover with a kitchen towel and let rest at room temperature, until the dough has doubled in size. Check the dough after 1 hour.

4. Transfer the dough to a floured work surface. Divide the dough into 2 equal pieces and roll each piece into a ball. Let rest on the floured work surface for 10 minutes.

5. Place the palms of the hands on one ball and roll it backward and forward until it forms an elongated shape, 10 inches long. Repeat the process with the other ball of dough.

6. Line a tray with a well-floured kitchen towel and place the loaves on top. Let rise until the dough has doubled in size, about 1 hour.

7. Meanwhile, place a pizza stone on the bottom rack of the oven and preheat to 450°F. Carefully transfer dough to a floured pizza paddle. Using a sharp knife, make 3 slashes, at an angle of 45 degrees, along the length of each loaf.

8. Use pizza paddle to carefully place the loaves 1-inch apart on the stone. Pour water in a ceramic cup or a heat-resistant container and place in the oven to generate steam during baking.

9. Bake at 450°F for 7 minutes. Then reduce heat to 400°F and bake for an additional 25-30 minutes. The bread is ready when a knock on the bottom produces a hollow sound.

10. Remove from oven. Allow to cool on a wire rack for 30 minutes before serving.

SWEET ANISE-SCENTED BAGUETTES

Preparation time: 30 min.
Resting time: 75 min.
Rising time: 1 hr.
Baking time: 22–25 min.

INGREDIENTS

1 cup water

1 oz. fresh yeast or $1^1/_2$ teaspoons
   active dry yeast

1 tablespoon anise seeds, coarsely
   ground

$^1/_2$ cup white sourdough starter
   (see page 20)

$^1/_2$ cup whole-wheat flour

2 cups bread flour

$1^1/_2$ teaspoons salt

Additional flour for assorted tasks

Special Tools
Ceramic cup or a heat-resistant
   container

PREPARATION

1. In the bowl of a standing electric mixer with the dough hook attached, mix the water, yeast, anise seeds, white sourdough starter and flours at low speed for 3 minutes. With the machine running, add the salt, switch to medium speed and continue kneading for an additional 7 minutes.

2. Place the dough in a greased bowl, cover with a kitchen towel and let rest at room temperature until the dough has doubled in size. Check the dough after 1 hour.

3. Transfer the dough to a floured work surface. Divide the dough into 3 equal pieces and roll each piece into a ball. Let rest on the floured work surface for 10 minutes.

4. Place the palms of the hands on one ball and roll it backward and forward until it is an elongated shape, 10 inches long. Repeat with the other pieces of dough. Let rest for 5 minutes.

5. Roll one piece of dough until it reaches a 20-inch long baguette shape with slightly tapered ends. Repeat with the other dough pieces.

6. Line a tray with a well-floured kitchen towel and place the baguettes on top.

7. Let rise until the dough has doubled in size, about 1 hour.

8. Meanwhile, place a pizza stone on the bottom rack of the oven and preheat to 450°F.

9. Carefully transfer dough to a floured pizza paddle. Using a sharp knife, make 5 slashes, at a 45-degree angle, along the length of each baguette.

10. Use pizza paddle to carefully place the baguettes 1-inch apart on the stone.

11. Pour water in a ceramic cup or a heat-resistant container and place in the oven to generate steam during baking.

12. Bake at 450°F for 7 minutes. Then reduce heat to 400°F and bake for an additional 15-18 minutes. The bread is ready when a knock on the bottom produces a hollow sound.

13. Remove from oven. Allow to cool on a wire rack for 30 minutes before serving.

This aromatic baguette has a delicate scent of anise, subtle enough not to overwhelm, yet present enough to refine the taste.

ZESTY ROASTED CORN & CHILI BREAD — CIABATTA STYLE

MAKES 2 LOAVES

Preparation time: 30 min.
Resting time: 1 hr.
Rising time: 1 hr.
Baking time: 32–35 min.

INGREDIENTS

1¹/₄ cups water

1 oz. fresh yeast or 1¹/₂ teaspoons
    active dry yeast

¹/₂ cup white sourdough starter
    (see page 20)

¹/₂ cup whole-wheat flour

2 cups bread flour

1¹/₂ teaspoons salt

2 tablespoons extra-virgin olive oil,
    for dough

2 tablespoons red chili, finely chopped

¹/₂ cup corn kernels, frozen

2 tablespoons extra-virgin olive oil,
    for greasing the bowl

Additional flour for assorted tasks

Special Tools
Ceramic cup or a heat-resistant
    container

PREPARATION

1. In the bowl of a standing electric mixer with the dough hook attached, mix the water, yeast, white sourdough starter and flours at low speed for 3 minutes. With the machine running, add the salt, switch to medium speed and continue kneading for an additional 2 minutes.

2. With the machine running, slowly drizzle in the olive oil and continue kneading until well blended.

3. Stop the machine. Add chopped chili and corn kernels and knead at low speed for 1 minute, until evenly distributed.

4. Grease a large bowl with 2 tablespoons of olive oil. Place the dough in the bowl, cover with kitchen towel and let rest at room temperature until the dough has doubled in size. Check the dough after 1 hour.

5. Transfer dough to a floured surface. Using a dough scraper or a knife, divide the dough in half. Shape into rectangles.

(continued on page 98)

¤ *Zesty Roasted Corn & Chili Bread — Ciabatta Style*

(continued from page 96)

6. Line a tray with a well-floured kitchen towel and place the loaves on top. Let rise until the dough has doubled in size, about 1 hour.

7. Meanwhile, place a pizza stone on the bottom rack of the oven and preheat to 450°F.

8. Carefully transfer dough to a floured pizza paddle. Using a sharp knife, make a slash along the length of each loaf.

9. Use pizza paddle to carefully place loaves 1-inch apart on the stone.

10. Pour water in a ceramic cup or a heat-resistant container and place in the oven to generate steam during baking.

11. Bake at 450°F for 7 minutes. Then reduce heat to 400°F and bake for an additional 25-28 minutes. The bread is ready when a knock on the bottom produces a hollow sound.

12. Remove from oven. Allow to cool on a wire rack for 30 minutes before serving.

The combination of corn and chili pepper creates a surprising flavor with each bite!

FLAVORFUL MEDITERRANEAN BAGELS

MAKES 12 BAGELS

Preparation time: 20 min.
Resting time: 70 min.
Rising time: 1¹/₂–2 hr.
Baking time: 18–20 min.

INGREDIENTS

1¹/₂ cups water

1 oz. fresh yeast or 1¹/₂ teaspoons
  active dry yeast

¹/₂ cup white sourdough starter
  (see page 20)

1 tablespoon extra-virgin olive oil,
  for dough

¹/₂ cup whole-wheat flour

3 cups bread flour

2 teaspoons salt

1 tablespoon fresh basil,
  finely chopped

1 tablespoon extra-virgin oil,
  for greasing the bowl

Garnish
1 cup raw sesame seeds

Additional flour for assorted tasks

PREPARATION

1. In the bowl of a standing electric mixer with the dough hook attached, mix the water, yeast, white sourdough starter, olive oil and flours at low speed for 3 minutes. With the machine running, add the salt and chopped basil, switch to medium speed and continue kneading for an additional 7 minutes.

2. Grease a medium bowl with 1 tablespoon of olive oil. Place the dough in the bowl, cover with plastic wrap or a large plastic bag and let rest until the dough has doubled in size. Check the dough after 1 hour.

3. Transfer the dough to a floured work surface. Using a dough scraper or a knife, divide the dough into 2 equal parts, then divide each part into 6 pieces to make a total of 12. Roll each piece into a ball. Let rest on the floured work surface for 10 minutes.

4. Prepare 2 separate deep bowls: Fill one with cold water and the other with sesame seeds.

5. Roll each ball into a log about 10 inches long. Dip each log in water and then roll in the sesame seeds, pressing gently so that the entire surface is evenly covered. Form the logs into circles by overlapping the ends ¹/₂-inch. Press the ring closed. Repeat the process with the remaining pieces of dough.

6. Holding two sides of each circle, stretch slightly into an oval shape.

7. Arrange the bagels 1-inch apart on a baking sheet lined with parchment paper.

8. Let rise in a warm place until the dough has doubled in size, about 1¹/₂-2 hours.

9. Preheat the oven to 425°F 40 minutes before the end of the rising time.

10. Once the bagels have risen, place them in the preheated oven. Then reduce heat to 400°F and bake the rolls for 18-20 minutes, or until golden brown and crispy.

11. Remove from oven. Allow to cool on a wire rack for 15 minutes before serving.

RICH
OLIVE
BREAD

MAKES 1 LOAF

Preparation time: 30 min.
Resting time: 1 hr.
Rising time: 1 hr.
Baking time: 32–37 min.

INGREDIENTS

$3/4$ cup water
1 oz. fresh yeast or $1^1/2$ teaspoons
   active dry yeast
1 cup bread flour
$1/2$ cup spelt flour
$1^1/2$ cups whole rye flour
1 teaspoon salt
$1/4$ cup Kalamata black olives, pitted
$1/4$ cup green French olives, pitted
2 tablespoons dried olives

Additional flour for assorted tasks

Special Tools
Ceramic cup or a heat-resistant
   container

PREPARATION

1. In the bowl of a standing electric mixer with the dough hook attached, mix the water, yeast and flours at low speed for 3 minutes. With the machine running, add the salt, switch to medium speed and continue kneading for an additional 6 minutes.

2. Stop the machine. Add Kalamata black olives, green French olives and dried olives and knead at low speed for 2 minutes, until well blended.

3. Place the dough in a large greased bowl, cover with a kitchen towel and let rest at room temperature, until the dough has doubled in size. Check the dough after 1 hour.

4. Transfer the dough to a floured work surface. Place the palms of both hands on the dough and roll it until it forms a ball.

5. Line a tray with a well-floured kitchen towel and place the dough on top. Let rise until the dough has doubled in size, about 1 hour.

6. Meanwhile, place a pizza stone on the bottom rack of the oven and preheat to 450°F.

7. Carefully transfer dough to a floured pizza paddle. Using a sharp knife, make 3 parallel slashes across the width of the bread. Turn the dough 90 degrees and make 3 more parallel slashes to create diamond-like shapes on the top of the bread.

8. Use pizza paddle to carefully place the dough on the stone. Pour water in a ceramic cup or a heat-resistant container and place in the oven to generate steam during baking.

9. Bake at 450°F for 7 minutes. Then reduce heat to 400°F and bake for an additional 25-30 minutes. The bread is ready when a knock on the bottom produces a hollow sound.

10. Remove from oven. Allow to cool on a wire rack for 30 minutes before serving.

¤ *Rich Olive Bread*

SEEDED CLASSIC CIABATTA

MAKES 4 ROLLS

Preparation time: 30 min.
Resting time: 1 hr.
Rising time: 1 hr.
Baking time: 24–26 min.

INGREDIENTS

2 tablespoons raw sesame seeds

2 tablespoons flax seeds

2 tablespoons sunflower seeds

1¼ cups water

1 oz. fresh yeast or 1½ teaspoons
   active dry yeast

⅓ cup white sourdough starter
   (see page 20)

½ cup whole-wheat flour

2 cups bread flour

1½ teaspoons salt

2 tablespoons extra-virgin olive oil,
   for the dough

2 tablespoons extra-virgin olive oil,
   for greasing the bowl

Water, for brushing

Additional flour for assorted tasks

Special Tools

Ceramic cup or a heat-resistant
   container

PREPARATION

1. In a small bowl, mix together the sesame, flax and sunflower seeds. Using a wooden spoon, stir until all seeds are mixed uniformly. Set aside 2 tablespoons of the seed mixture.

2. In the bowl of a standing electric mixer with the dough hook attached, mix the water, yeast, white sourdough starter and flours at low speed for 3 minutes. With the machine running, add the salt, switch to medium speed and knead for an additional 2 minutes.

3. With the machine running, slowlly drizzle the olive oil and beat until well blended.

4. Stop the machine. Add 4 tablespoons of the seed mixture (prepared in Step 1) and knead at low speed for 1 minute, until evenly distributed.

5. Grease a large bowl with 2 tablespoons of olive oil. Place the dough in the bowl, cover with kitchen towel and let rest at room temperature until the dough has doubled in size. Check the dough after 1 hour.

6. Using a dough scraper or a knife, divide the dough into 4 equal pieces. Shape into rectangles. Brush with water and sprinkle with remaining seed mixture (prepared in Step 1). Line a tray with a floured kitchen towel and place the pieces of dough on top. Let rise until the dough has doubled in size, about 1 hour.

7. Meanwhile, place a pizza stone on the bottom rack of the oven and preheat to 450°F. Carefully transfer dough to a floured pizza paddle. Use pizza paddle to carefully place the rolls 1-inch apart on the stone.

8. Pour water in a ceramic cup or a heat-resistant container and place in the oven to generate steam during baking.

9. Bake at 450°F for 7 minutes. Then, reduce heat to 400°F, and bake for an additional 17-19 minutes. The bread is ready when a knock on the bottom produces a hollow sound.

10. Remove from oven. Allow to cool on a wire rack for 30 minutes before serving.

¤ *Seeded Classic Ciabatta*

SWEET CHILI & CILANTRO BREAD

MAKES 1 LOAF

Preparation time: 30 min.
Resting time: 1 hr.
Rising time: 1 hr.
Baking time: 30–35 min.

INGREDIENTS

1 cup water

$1/_3$ cup Asian sweet chili sauce

1 oz. fresh yeast or $1^1/_2$ teaspoons active dry yeast

$1/_3$ cup dark sourdough starter (see page 19)

$1/_2$ cup whole-wheat flour

2 cups bread flour

$1^1/_2$ teaspoons salt

2 tablespoons extra-virgin olive oil, for dough

$1/_3$ cup fresh cilantro leaves, coarsely chopped

2 tablespoons extra-virgin olive oil, for greasing the bowl

Additional flour for assorted tasks

Special Tools

Ceramic cup or a heat-resistant container

This bread is a celebration of sweet and piquant tastes from the Far East. Cilantro leaves and sweet chili sauce gives it a surprising flavor.

PREPARATION

1. In the bowl of a standing electric mixer with the dough hook attached, mix the water, chili sauce, yeast, dark sourdough starter and flours, at low speed for 3 minutes. With the machine running, add the salt, switch to medium speed and continue kneading for an additional 2 minutes.

2. With the machine running, slowly drizzle the olive oil, beat until well blended.

3. Stop the machine. Add chopped cilantro leaves and knead at low speed for 1 minute, until evenly distributed.

4. Grease a medium bowl with 2 tablespoons of olive oil. Place the dough in bowl, cover with kitchen towel and let rest until the dough has doubled in size. Check the dough after 1 hour.

5. Transfer dough to a floured surface and roll into a ball. Place the ball on a baking sheet lined with parchment paper. Gently flatten the dough with your palm into a thin circle, 8 inches in diameter.

6. Let rise until the dough has doubled in size, about 1 hour. Meanwhile, place a pizza stone on the bottom rack of the oven and preheat to 450°F.

7. Use pizza paddle to carefully place the bread on the stone. Pour water in a ceramic cup or in a heat-resistant container and place it inside the oven to generate steam throughout the baking process.

8. Bake at 450°F for 5 minutes. Then reduce heat to 400°F and bake for an additional 25-30 minutes. The bread is ready when a knock on the bottom produces a hollow sound.

9. Remove from oven. Allow to cool on a wire rack for 30 minutes before serving.

THREE-COLOR SESAME ROLLS

MAKES 12 ROLLS

Preparation time: 20 min.
Resting time: 70 min.
Rising time: 1 hr.
Baking time: 18–20 min.

INGREDIENTS

1 1/2 cups water

1 oz. fresh yeast or 1 1/2 teaspoons
   active dry yeast

1/2 cup dark sourdough starter
   (see page 19)

2 tablespoons extra-virgin olive oil,
   for dough

1 cup whole-wheat flour

2 1/2 cups bread flour

2 teaspoons salt

1/4 cup raw sesame seeds

1/4 cup black sesame seeds

1/4 cup brown sesame seeds

1 tablespoon extra-virgin olive oil,
   for greasing the bowl

Additional flour for assorted tasks

Special Tools
Ceramic cup or a heat-resistant
   container

Triple the goodness with these fiber-enriched rolls. In addition to their unique crunchy texture, all three types of sesame seeds are packed with healthy benefits.

PREPARATION

1. In the bowl of a standing electric mixer with the dough hook attached, mix the water, yeast, dark sourdough starter, olive oil and flours, at low speed for 3 minutes. With the machine running, add the salt, switch to medium speed and continue kneading for an additional 5 minutes.

2. Stop the machine. Add raw, black and brown sesame seeds and knead at low speed for 2 minutes, until blended.

3. Grease a medium bowl with 1 tablespoon of olive oil. Place the dough in bowl, cover with a kitchen towel and let rest at room temperature until the dough has doubled in size. Check the dough after 1 hour.

4. Transfer the dough to a floured work surface. Divide the dough into 2 equal parts, then divide each part into 6 pieces to make a total of 12. Roll each piece into a ball. Let rest on the floured work surface for 10 minutes.

5. Place the rolls 1/2-inch apart on a baking sheet lined with parchment paper. Let rise in a warm place until the dough has doubled in size, about 1 hour.

6. Preheat the oven to 425°F 40 minutes before the end of the rising time.

7. Pour water in a ceramic cup or in a heat-resistant container and place it inside the oven to generate steam throughout the baking process.

8. Once the rolls have risen, place them in the preheated oven. Then reduce heat to 400°F and bake for 18-20 minutes, or until golden brown.

9. Remove from oven. Allow to cool on a wire rack for 15 minutes before serving.

SPECIAL
BREADS

IN THIS CHAPTER, YOU WILL FIND A VARIETY OF BREADS THAT WILL INTRODUCE YOU TO NEW AND DIFFERENT INGREDIENT COMBINATIONS. IT IS IMPORTANT TO HAVE THE HIGHEST-QUALITY INGREDIENTS BEFORE YOU START. TAKE A FEW MINUTES TO FAMILIARIZE YOURSELF WITH THE RECIPE. YOU'LL WANT TO UNDERSTAND THE NECESSARY STEPS SO YOU CAN PLAN AND CORRECTLY PREPARE FOR THE BAKING PROCESS, INCLUDING RESTING, RISING AND COOLING TIMES. THIS WILL HELP ENSURE GREATER SUCCESS IN YOUR BAKING.

THE VARIETY OF BREADS IN THIS CHAPTER OFFER A WIDE RANGE OF RECIPES FOR HOSTING FRIENDS AND FAMILY OR JUST AS A PERSONAL INDULGENCE TO SATISFY YOUR CRAVING FOR FRESH BREAD. SERVE AS AN ADDITION TO ANY MEAL OR WITH JUST A SALAD FOR A LIGHTER MEAL. ALL THE RECIPES ARE SUITABLE FOR BAKING IN THE HOME KITCHEN AND WILL SURELY LEAVE A COZY AND HOMEY SCENT!

ITALIAN WALNUT BREAD

MAKES 1 LOAF

Preparation time: 30 min.
Resting time: 1 hr.
Rising time: 1^1/$_2$ hr.
Baking time: 40 min.

INGREDIENTS

1^1/$_3$ cups water

1 oz. fresh yeast or 1^1/$_2$ teaspoons
    active dry yeast

^{1}/$_2$ cup white sourdough starter
    (see page 20)

1 tablespoon extra-virgin olive oil,
    for dough

2 cups bread flour

1 cup whole-wheat flour

^{1}/$_2$ cup rye flour

2 tablespoons salt

^{1}/$_4$ cup ground hazelnuts

^{1}/$_4$ cup walnuts, chopped

^{1}/$_4$ cup almonds, coarsely ground

1 tablespoon extra-virgin olive oil,
    for greasing the bowl

Additional flour for assorted tasks

Special Tools
Ceramic cup or a heat-resistant
    container

PREPARATION

1. In the bowl of a standing electric mixer with the dough hook attached, mix the water, yeast, white sourdough starter, olive oil and flours at low speed for 3 minutes. With the machine running, add the salt, switch to medium speed and continue kneading for an additional 6 minutes.

2. Stop the machine. Add the hazelnuts, walnuts and almonds and knead at low speed for 2 minutes, until well blended.

3. Grease a medium bowl with 1 tablespoon of olive oil. Place the dough in the bowl, cover with kitchen towel and let rest until the dough has doubled in size. Check the dough after 1 hour.

4. Transfer the dough to a floured work surface. Place the palms of both hands on the dough and roll it until it forms a ball.

5. Line a wide bowl with a well-floured kitchen towel and place the dough inside.

6. Cover with kitchen towel and let rise in a warm place until the dough has doubled in size, about 1^1/$_2$ hours.

7. Meanwhile, place a pizza stone on the bottom rack of the oven and preheat to 450°F.

8. Once the dough has risen, carefully turn the dough over on a floured work surface.

9. Use pizza paddle to slide the bread onto the stone.

10. Pour water in a ceramic cup or in a heat-resistant container and place it inside the oven to generate steam throughout the baking process.

11. Bake 450°F for 10 minutes. Then reduce heat to 375°F and bake for an additional 30 minutes. The bread is ready when a knock on the bottom produces a hollow sound.

12. Remove from oven. Allow to cool on a wire rack for 30 minutes before serving.

WHOLE-GRAIN CARROT BREAD

MAKES 1 LOAF

Preparation time: 30 min.
Resting time: 1 hr.
Rising time: 1 hr.
Baking time: 40 min.

INGREDIENTS

1¼ cups water

1 oz. fresh yeast or 1½ teaspoons
   active dry yeast

⅓ cup white sourdough starter (see
   page 20)

1 tablespoon honey

2 cups whole-wheat flour

1½ cups bread flour

2 teaspoons salt

2 tablespoons rolled oats

1 tablespoon flax seeds

1 tablespoon sesame seeds

3 large carrots, peeled, finely grated

1 tablespoon extra-virgin olive oil,
   for greasing the bowl

Additional flour for assorted tasks

Special Tools
Ceramic cup or a heat-resistant
   container

Begin your day with this wonderful bread. It is tasty and nutritious and best for healthy sandwiches, French toast and weekend brunch.

PREPARATION

1. In the bowl of a standing electric mixer with the dough hook attached, mix the water, yeast, white sourdough starter, honey and flours at low speed for 3 minutes. With the machine running, add the salt, switch to medium speed and continue kneading for an additional 6 minutes.

2. Stop the machine. Add rolled oats, flax seeds, sesame seeds and grated carrots and knead at low speed for 2 minutes, until well blended.

3. Grease a medium bowl with the olive oil. Place the dough in the bowl, cover with kitchen towel and let rest until the dough has doubled in size. Check the dough after 1 hour.

4. Transfer the dough to a floured work surface. Place the palms of the hands on one ball and roll it backward and forward to form a cylinder, 10 inches long.

5. Place the dough on a floured work surface. Cover with kitchen towel and let rise in a warm place until the dough has doubled in size, about 1 hour. Meanwhile, place a pizza stone on the bottom rack of the oven and preheat to 425°F.

6. Once the dough has risen, carefully transfer dough to a floured pizza paddle. Using a sharp knife to make 2 diagonal slashes from the right side and 2 diagonal slashes from the left side, creating a diamond-like shape on top.

7. Use pizza paddle to carefully place the dough on the stone. Pour water in a ceramic cup or in a heat-resistant container and place it inside the oven to generate steam throughout the baking process.

8. Bake at 425°F for 5 minutes. Then reduce heat to 375°F and bake for an additional 35 minutes.

9. Remove from oven. Allow to cool completely on a wire rack for 30 minutes before serving.

¤ *Whole-Grain Carrot Bread*

EARTHY SEED LOAF

MAKES 1 LOAF

Preparation time: 30 min.
Resting time: 2 hr.
Rising time: 2 hr.
Baking time: 50 min.

INGREDIENTS

2 cups lukewarm water
1 oz. fresh yeast or 1^1/$_2$ teaspoons
   active dry yeast
^{1}/$_2$ cup dark sourdough starter
   (see p. 19)
1 tablespoon honey
^{1}/$_2$ cup whole-wheat flour
^{1}/$_2$ cup brown sesame seeds
^{1}/$_2$ tablespoon flax seeds
^{1}/$_2$ cup poppy seeds
^{1}/$_2$ cup sunflower seeds
^{1}/$_2$ cup pumpkin seeds
1 cup rolled oats
2 teaspoons salt

Additional flour for assorted tasks

Special Tools
Nonstick 5 x 9-inch loaf pan
Ceramic cup or a heat-resistant
   container

Bakers often call this type of bread "pound cake". It contains a very small amount of flour and is still tasty and nutritious. One delightful variation is to serve it stuffed with smoked salmon or cheese.

PREPARATION

1. In the bowl of a standing electric mixer with the flat beater attached, mix the water, yeast, dark sourdough starter, honey, whole-wheat flour, brown sesame, flax, poppy, sunflower and pumpkin seeds, rolled oats and salt at low speed for 10 minutes.

2. Cover with plastic wrap or a large plastic bag and let rest in a warm place until the dough has doubled in size. Check the dough after about 2 hours.

3. Sprinkle a little flour on top, carefully remove the dough from bowl and place it on a floured work surface. Add flour to your hands to keep them from sticking to the dough and roll into a cylinder. Be sure to add a small amount of flour as you knead the dough.

4. Place the dough in the loaf pan, cover with kitchen towel and let rise in a warm place until the dough has doubled in size, about 2 hours.

5. Preheat oven to 425°F.

6. Pour water in a ceramic cup or in a heat-resistant container and place it inside the oven to generate steam throughout the baking process.

7. Bake at 425°F for 15 minutes. Then reduce heat to 375°F and bake for an additional 35 minutes.

8. Remove from oven. Allow to cool completely on a wire rack for at least 3 hours before serving. Be sure the bread has cooled completely before slicing.

¤ *Earthy Seed Loaf*

DECADENT FIG & GOAT CHEESE STUFFED BREAD

MAKES 1 LOAF

Preparation time: 30 min.
Resting time: 1 hr.
Rising time: 1 hr.
Baking time: 35 min.

INGREDIENTS

1 1/3 cups water

1 oz. fresh yeast or 1 1/2 teaspoons
   active dry yeast

1/2 cup white sourdough starter
   (see page 20)

2 cups bread flour

1 1/2 cups whole-wheat flour

2 teaspoons salt

8 oz. goat cheese, crumbled

8 large ripe figs, cut into quarters

Additional flour for assorted tasks

Special Tools

Ceramic cup or a heat-resistant
   container

The combination of figs and goat cheese add an interesting surprise with a gourmet meal; a must-have when you are hosting. The figs are high in natural sugar, but a good source of fiber and contains important minerals.

PREPARATION

1. In the bowl of a standing electric mixer with the dough hook attached, mix the water, yeast, white sourdough starter and flours at low speed for 3 minutes. With the machine running, add the salt, switch to medium speed and continue kneading for an additional 7 minutes.

2. Place the dough in a medium greased bowl, cover with a kitchen towel and let rest until the dough has doubled in size. Check the dough after 1 hour.

3. Place the dough on a floured work surface. Using a lightly floured rolling pin, roll the dough into an 8 x 12-inch rectangle.

4. Spread the goat cheese on the dough and arrange the figs on top.

5. Roll the dough jellyroll style, ensuring that all the filling is inside. Press to flatten the roll slightly.

6. Place the loaf on a baking sheet lined with parchment paper and let rise in a warm place until the dough has doubled in size, about 1 hour.

7. Preheat oven to 425°F.

8. Once the dough has risen, transfer the baking sheet to the preheated oven.

9. Pour water in a ceramic cup or in a heat-resistant container and place it inside the oven to generate steam throughout the baking process.

10. Bake at 425°F for 10 minutes. Then reduce heat to 375°F and bake for an additional 25 minutes, until dark brown.

11. Remove from oven. Allow to cool on a wire rack for 30 minutes before serving.

YELLOW CHEESE & WILD MUSHROOM BREAD

MAKES 1 LOAF

Preparation time: 30 min.
Resting time: 1 hr.
Rising time: 1 hr.
Baking time: 40 min.

INGREDIENTS

1$\frac{1}{3}$ cups water

1 oz. fresh yeast or 1$\frac{1}{2}$ teaspoons active dry yeast

$\frac{1}{2}$ cup dark sourdough starter (see page 19)

1 cup bread flour

1 cup rye flour

1$\frac{1}{2}$ cups whole-wheat flour

2 teaspoons salt

4 oz. Gouda cheese, shredded

4 oz. Cheddar cheese, shredded

$\frac{1}{2}$ cup fresh white mushrooms, sliced

Additional flour for assorted tasks

Special Tools
Ceramic cup or a heat-resistant container

This bread is very suitable for hosting or for a cozy family dinner. The cheese and mushrooms turn this bread into a dish that can stand alone as a meal. Add some salad and it will definitely satisfy as a light meal.

PREPARATION

1. In the bowl of a standing electric mixer with the dough hook attached, mix the water, yeast, dark sourdough starter and flours at low speed for 3 minutes. With the machine running, add the salt, switch to medium speed and continue kneading for an additional 7 minutes.

2. Place the dough in a medium greased bowl, cover with a kitchen towel and let rest until the dough has doubled in size. Check the dough after 1 hour.

3. Place the dough on a floured work surface. Using the palms of the hands, flatten the dough to form an 8 x 12-inch rectangle.

4. Spread the Gouda and Cheddar cheese on the dough and arrange the mushrooms on top.

5. Roll the dough jellyroll style, ensuring that all the filling is inside. Press to flatten the roll slightly.

6. Place the roll on a baking sheet lined with parchment paper and let rise in a warm place until the dough has doubled in size, about 1 hour.

7. Preheat oven to 425°F. Once the dough has risen, transfer the baking sheet to the preheated oven.

8. Pour water in a ceramic cup or in a heat-resistant container and place it inside the oven to generate steam throughout the baking process.

9. Bake at 425°F for 10 minutes. Then reduce heat to 375°F and bake for an additional 30 minutes.

10. Remove from oven. Allow to cool on a wire rack for 30 minutes before serving.

SPICED CHEESE & NUT BREAD

MAKES 2 LOAVES

Preparation time: 30 min.
Resting time: 1 hr.
Rising time: 1 hr.
Baking time: 40–42 min.

INGREDIENTS

1$^1/_3$ cups water

1 oz. fresh yeast or 1$^1/_2$ teaspoons
   active dry yeast

$^1/_2$ cup dark sourdough starter
   (see page 19)

1 cup bread flour

1 cup rye flour

1$^1/_2$ cups whole-wheat flour

2 teaspoons salt

$^3/_4$ pound blue cheese, coarsely
   crumbled

$^1/_2$ pound walnuts, coarsely ground

Additional flour for assorted tasks

Special Tools
Ceramic cup or a heat-resistant
   container

This spicy bread can be a prefect serving as part of any meal.
It is also a comfort food on a cold winter day.

PREPARATION

1. In the bowl of a standing electric mixer with the dough hook attached, mix the water, yeast, dark sourdough starter and flours at low speed for 3 minutes. With the machine running, add the salt, switch to medium speed and continue kneading for an additional 5 minutes.

2. Stop the machine. Add the blue cheese and ground walnuts and knead at low speed for 2 minutes, until well blended.

3. Place the dough in a medium greased bowl, cover with a kitchen towel and let rest until the dough has doubled in size. Check the dough after 1 hour.

4. Transfer the dough to a floured work surface. Using the palms of the hands, flatten the dough to form a 6 x 10-inch rectangle.

5. Using a sharp knife, slice the dough into 2 equal rectangles, 5 x 6-inches each.

6. Place the pieces of dough on floured kitchen towel and let rise in a warm place until the dough has doubled in size, about 1 hour.

7. Meanwhile, place a pizza stone on the bottom rack of the oven and preheat to 450°F. Once the dough has risen, carefully transfer dough to a floured work surface. Use pizza paddle to slide the loaves onto the stone, 2-inches apart.

8. Pour water in a ceramic cup or in a heat-resistant container and place it inside the oven to generate steam throughout the baking process.

9. Bake at 450°F for 5 minutes. Then reduce heat to 400°F and bake for an additional 35-37 minutes. The bread is ready when a knock on the bottom produces a hollow sound.

10. Remove from oven. Allow to cool on a wire rack for 30 minutes before serving.

PRUNE & PORT WHOLE-WHEAT BREAD

MAKES 1 LOAF

Preparation time: 30 min.
Resting time: 1 hr.
Rising time: 1 hr.
Baking time: 40 min.

INGREDIENTS

$^1/_4$ cup port wine

$^1/_2$ cup prunes, pitted and halved

1 cup water

1 oz. fresh yeast or $1^1/_2$ teaspoons
   active dry yeast

$^1/_3$ cup dark sourdough starter
   (see page 19)

1 tablespoon honey

2 cups whole-wheat flour

$1^1/_2$ cups bread flour

2 teaspoons salt

1 tablespoon extra-virgin olive oil,
   for greasing the bowl

Additional flour for assorted tasks

Special Tools
Nonstick 5 x 9-inch loaf pan
Ceramic cup or a heat-resistant
   container

This bread is slightly sweet because of the combination of the port and the prunes. Spoil your guests with bread they won't forget. Best served alongside dishes from the Spanish or southern French kitchens.

PREPARATION

1. Soak the prunes in a bowl of port wine for at least 2 hours before using. Strain and reserve the prunes and syrup separately.

2. In the bowl of a standing electric mixer with the dough hook attached, mix the water, yeast, dark sourdough starter, honey, port syrup (prepared in Step 1) and flours at low speed for 3 minutes. With the machine running, add the salt, switch to medium speed and continue kneading for an additional 6 minutes.

3. Stop the machine. Add the prunes (prepared in Step 1) and knead at low speed for 2 minutes, until well blended.

4. Grease a medium bowl with the olive oil. Place the dough in the bowl, cover with kitchen towel and let rest until the dough has doubled in size. Check the dough after 1 hour.

5. Transfer the dough to a floured work surface. Place the palms of the hands on the ball of dough and roll it backward and forward to form a cylinder, 9 inches long.

6. Place the dough in the loaf pan and flatten it out with the palm of the hand until it fits snugly.

7. Cover with kitchen towel and let rise in a warm place until the dough has doubled in size, about 1 hour. Preheat oven to 425°F. Once the dough has risen, transfer the loaf pan to the preheated oven.

8. Pour water in a ceramic cup or in a heat-resistant container and place it inside the oven to generate steam throughout the baking process.

9. Bake at 425°F for 5 minutes. Then reduce heat to 375°F and bake for an additional 35 minutes.

10. Remove from oven. Allow to cool on a wire rack for 30 minutes before serving.

¤ *Prune & Port Whole-Wheat Bread*

CLASSIC GERMAN RYE BREAD

MAKES 1 LOAF

Preparation time: 30 min.
Resting time: 1 hr.
Rising time: 1¹/₂ hr.
Baking time: 45 min.

INGREDIENTS

1¹/₃ cups water

1 oz. fresh yeast or 1¹/₂ teaspoons
    active dry yeast

¹/₃ cup dark sourdough starter
    (see page 19)

1 tablespoon honey

2 cups whole-wheat flour

1¹/₂ cups rye flour

2 teaspoons salt

1 tablespoon extra-virgin olive oil,
    for greasing the bowl

Additional flour for assorted tasks

Special Tools
Ceramic cup or a heat-resistant
    container

This black German rye bread has a tangy flavor perfectly suited for rich sandwiches. Spread it with a layer of butter and add a few slices of your favorite hard cheese. In any form, it will taste simply wonderful!

PREPARATION

1. In the bowl of a standing electric mixer with the dough hook attached, mix the water, yeast, dark sourdough starter, honey and flours at low speed for 3 minutes. With the machine running, add the salt, switch to medium speed and continue kneading for an additional 7 minutes.

2. Grease a medium bowl with the olive oil. Place the dough in the bowl, cover with kitchen towel and let rest until the dough has doubled in size. Check the dough after 1 hour.

3. Transfer the dough to a floured work surface. Place the palms of both hands on the dough and roll it until it forms a ball.

4. Line a bowl with a well-floured kitchen towel and place the dough inside.

5. Let rise in a warm place until the dough has doubled in size, about 1¹/₂ hours.

6. Meanwhile, place a pizza stone on the bottom rack of the oven and preheat to 425°F.

7. Once the dough has risen, carefully turn the dough over on a floured work surface. Use pizza paddle to slide the bread onto the stone.

8. Pour water in a ceramic cup or in a heat-resistant container and place it inside the oven to generate steam throughout the baking process.

9. Bake 425°F for 10 minutes. Then reduce heat to 375°F and bake for an additional 35 minutes. The bread is ready when a knock on the bottom produces a hollow sound.

10. Remove from oven. Allow to cool on a wire rack for 30 minutes before serving.

¤ *Classic German Rye Bread*

UNIQUE WINTRY CHESTNUT BREAD

MAKES 1 LOAF

Preparation time: 30 min.
Resting time: 1 hr.
Rising time: 1 hr.
Baking time: 40 min.

INGREDIENTS

1$^1/_3$ cups milk

1 oz. fresh yeast or 1$^1/_2$ teaspoons
   active dry yeast

$^1/_2$ cup white sourdough starter
   (see page 20)

2 tablespoons chestnut paste

1 cup bread flour

1 cup rye flour

1$^1/_2$ cups whole-wheat flour

2 teaspoons salt

1 cup vacuum-packed chestnuts,
   peeled

1 tablespoon extra-virgin olive oil,
   for greasing the bowl

Additional flour for assorted tasks

Special Tools
Ceramic cup or a heat-resistant
   container

Chestnut enthusiasts, beware — this bread is very addictive!
When you mark it with the baker's "signature", be sure to make
4 slashes instead of 2. Cutting 2 slashes will distort its round shape.

PREPARATION

1. In the bowl of a standing electric mixer with the dough hook attached, mix the milk, yeast, white sourdough starter, chestnut paste and flours at low speed for 3 minutes. With the machine running, add the salt, switch to medium speed and continue kneading for an additional 6 minutes.

2. Stop the machine. Add the peeled chestnuts and knead at low speed for 2 minutes, until well blended.

3. Grease a medium bowl with the olive oil. Place the dough in the bowl, cover with kitchen towel and let rest until the dough has doubled in size. Check the dough after 1 hour. Transfer the dough to a floured work surface. Place the palms of both hands on the dough and roll it until it forms a ball.

4. Line a large bowl with a well-floured kitchen towel and place the dough inside. Cover with kitchen towel and let rise in a warm place until the dough has doubled in size, about 1 hour.

5. Meanwhile, place a pizza stone on the bottom rack of the oven and preheat to 450°F. Once the dough has risen, carefully transfer dough to a floured work surface. Using a sharp knife, make 4 slashes running from the center outwards to form a cross-like shape.

6. Use pizza paddle to slide the bread onto the stone, with the slashes facing up.

7. Pour water in a ceramic cup or in a heat-resistant container and place it inside the oven to generate steam throughout the baking process.

8. Bake at 450°F for 5 minutes. Then reduce heat to 400°F and bake for an additional 35 minutes. The bread is ready when a knock on the bottom produces a hollow sound.

9. Remove from oven. Allow to cool on a wire rack for 30 minutes before serving.

HONEY-LEMON BREAD

MAKES 1 LOAF

Preparation time: 30 min.
Resting time: 1 hr.
Rising time: 1 hr.
Baking time: 40 min.

INGREDIENTS

1 cup water

1 oz. fresh yeast or 1 1/2 teaspoons active dry yeast

1/3 cup white sourdough starter (see page 20)

2 tablespoons honey

Zest of 1 lemon

Juice of 1 lemon

2 cups whole-wheat flour

1 cup bread flour

1/2 cup rye flour

2 teaspoons salt

1 tablespoon extra-virgin olive oil, for greasing the bowl

Additional flour for assorted tasks

Special Tools

Nonstick 5 x 9-inch loaf pan

Ceramic cup or a heat-resistant container

I adore lemons. I have two trees growing in my yard and enjoy their fruits throughout the entire year. This bread has a delicate touch to it, fragrant from the combination of honey and lemon.

PREPARATION

1. In the bowl of a standing electric mixer with the dough hook attached, mix the water, yeast, white sourdough starter, honey, lemon zest, lemon juice and flours at low speed for 3 minutes. With the machine running, add the salt, switch to medium speed and continue kneading for an additional 7 minutes.

2. Grease a medium bowl with the olive oil. Place the dough in the bowl, cover with kitchen towel and let rest until the dough has doubled in size. Check the dough after 1 hour.

3. Transfer the dough to a floured work surface. Place the palms of the hands on the ball of dough and roll it backward and forward to form a cylinder, 10 inches long.

4. Place the dough in the loaf pan and flatten it out with the palm of the hand until it fits snugly.

5. Cover with kitchen towel and let rise in a warm place until the dough has doubled in size, about 1 hour.

6. Preheat oven to 425°F.

7. Once the dough has risen, transfer the loaf pan into the preheated oven.

8. Pour water in a ceramic cup or in a heat-resistant container and place it inside the oven to generate steam throughout the baking process.

9. Bake at 425°F for 5 minutes. Then reduce heat to 375°F and bake for an additional 35 minutes.

10. Remove from oven. Allow to cool on a wire rack for 30 minutes before serving.

HAZELNUT BREAD

MAKES 1 LOAF

Preparation time: 30 min.
Resting time: 1 hr.
Rising time: 1¹/₂ hr.
Baking time: 40 min.

INGREDIENTS

1¹/₃ cups water

1 oz. fresh yeast or 1¹/₂ teaspoons
   active dry yeast

¹/₂ cup dark sourdough starter
   (see page 19)

2 cups bread flour

1¹/₂ cups whole-wheat flour

2 teaspoons salt

¹/₂ cup ground hazelnuts

1 tablespoon extra-virgin olive oil,
   for greasing the bowl

Garnish

1 tablespoon ground hazelnuts

Additional flour for assorted tasks

Special Tools

Ceramic cup or a heat-resistant
   container

PREPARATION

1. In the bowl of a standing electric mixer with the dough hook attached, mix the water, yeast, dark sourdough starter and flours at low speed for 3 minutes. With the machine running, add the salt, switch to medium speed and continue kneading for an additional 6 minutes.

2. Stop the machine. Add ¹/₂ cup of ground hazelnuts and knead at low speed for 2 minutes, until well blended.

3. Grease a medium bowl with the olive oil. Place the dough in the bowl, cover with kitchen towel and let rest until the dough has doubled in size. Check the dough after 1 hour.

4. Transfer the dough to a floured work surface. Place the palms of both hands on the dough and roll it until it forms a ball.

5. Line a large bowl with a kitchen towel and sprinkle 1 tablespoon of ground hazelnuts and a little flour on towel. Place the dough inside. Cover with kitchen towel and let rise in a warm place until the dough has doubled in size, about 1¹/₂ hours.

6. Meanwhile, place a pizza stone on the bottom rack of the oven and preheat to 450°F. Once the dough has risen, carefully transfer dough to a floured surface. Using a sharp knife, make 6 slashes, starting from the center of the ball and working your way outwards to create a flower-like design.

7. Use pizza paddle to slide the bread onto the stone with the slashes facing up. Pour water in a ceramic cup or in a heat-resistant container and place it inside the oven to generate steam throughout the baking process.

8. Bake at 450°F for 5 minutes. Then reduce heat to 400°F and bake for an additional 35 minutes. The bread is ready when a knock on the bottom produces a hollow sound.

9. Remove from oven. Allow to cool completely on a wire rack for 30 minutes before serving.

COUNTRY BREAD WITH WAKAME SEAWEED

MAKES 1 LOAF

Preparation time: 30 min.
Resting time: 1 hr.
Rising time: 1^1/$_2$ hr.
Baking time: 45 min.

INGREDIENTS

1^1/$_3$ cups water

3 tablespoons Japanese dried
   Wakame seaweed

1 oz. fresh yeast or 1^1/$_2$ teaspoons
   active dry yeast

^{1}/$_3$ cup dark sourdough starter
   (see page 19)

1 cup whole-wheat flour

1^1/$_2$ cups bread flour

1 cup rye flour

2 teaspoons salt

1 tablespoon extra-virgin olive oil,
   for greasing the bowl

Additional flour for assorted tasks

Special Tools
Ceramic cup or a heat-resistant
   container

I first had this type of bread thirteen years ago in Cancale, a small town in France. I will never forget this as the best seafood meal I have ever eaten. This bread is best served with fish and seafood meals.

PREPARATION

1. In a small bowl, soak the seaweed in water for 20 minutes or until it swells.

2. In the bowl of a standing electric mixer with the dough hook attached, mix the seaweed with liquid, yeast, dark sourdough starter and flours, at low speed for 3 minutes. With the machine running, add the salt, switch to medium speed and continue kneading for an additional 7 minutes.

3. Grease a medium bowl with the olive oil. Place the dough in the bowl, cover with kitchen towel and let rest until the dough has doubled in size. Check the dough after 1 hour. Transfer the dough to a floured work surface. Place the palms of both hands on the dough and roll it until it forms a ball.

4. Line a large bowl with a well-floured kitchen towel and place the dough inside. Let rise in a warm place until the dough has doubled in size, about 1^1/$_2$ hours.

5. Meanwhile, place a pizza stone on the bottom rack of the oven and preheat to 450°F. Once the dough has risen, carefully transfer dough to a floured work surface. Using a sharp knife, make 4 slashes, starting from the center of the ball to create a square shape.

6. Use pizza paddle to slide the bread onto the stone. Pour water in a ceramic cup or in a heat-resistant container and place it inside the oven to generate steam throughout the baking process.

7. Bake at 450°F for 10 minutes. Then reduce heat to 375°F and bake for an additional 35 minutes. The bread is ready when a knock on the bottom produces a hollow sound.

8. Remove from oven. Allow to cool on a wire rack for 30 minutes before serving.

¤ *Country Bread with Wakame Seaweed*

EGGPLANT & CACIOTTA CHEESE BREAD

MAKES 2 LOAVES

Preparation time: 30 min.
Resting time: 1 hr.
Rising time: 1 hr.
Baking time: 40 min.

INGREDIENTS

2 medium eggplants, sliced lengthwise into strips, $1/2$-inch thick, with peel

2 tablespoons extra-virgin olive oil

$1/2$ teaspoon salt, for seasoning

$1^{1}/_{3}$ cups water

1 oz. fresh yeast or $1^{1}/_{2}$ teaspoons active dry yeast

$1/2$ cup dark sourdough starter (see p. 19)

1 cup bread flour

1 cup rye flour

$1^{1}/_{2}$ cups whole-wheat flour

2 teaspoons salt

12 oz. caciotta cheese, shredded

Additional flour for assorted tasks

Special Tools

Ceramic cup or a heat-resistant container

PREPARATION

1. Preheat oven to 425°F.

2. Arrange eggplant slices $1/2$-inch apart on a baking pan lined with parchment paper. Brush with olive oil and sprinkle salt on top. Bake for 12 minutes or until golden. Set aside for later use.

3. In the bowl of a standing electric mixer with the dough hook attached, mix the water, yeast, dark sourdough starter and flours at low speed for 3 minutes. With the machine running, add the salt, switch to medium speed and continue kneading for an additional 7 minutes.

4. Place the dough in a medium greased bowl, cover with a kitchen towel and let rest until the dough has doubled in size. Check the dough after 1 hour.

5. Place the dough on a floured work surface. Using a lightly floured rolling pin, roll the dough into an 8 x 10-inch rectangle.

6. Spread the caciotta cheese on the dough and arrange the roasted eggplant slices on top. Roll the dough jellyroll style, ensuring that all the filling is inside.

7. Using a sharp knife, divide the roll into 2 equal halves. Place each half on their flat side on a baking sheet lined with parchment paper, leaving 5 inches between each half.

8. Let rise in a warm place until the dough has doubled in size, about 1 hour.

9. Preheat oven to 425°F. Once the dough has risen, transfer the baking sheet to the preheated oven.

10. Pour water in a ceramic cup or in a heat-resistant container and place it inside the oven to generate steam throughout the baking process.

11. Bake at 425°F for 10 minutes. Then reduce heat to 375°F and bake for an additional 30 minutes.

12. Remove from oven. Allow to cool on a wire rack for 30 minutes before serving.

¤ *Eggplant & Caciotta Cheese Bread*

GARLIC CONFIT FOCACCIA

MAKES 1 LOAF

Preparation time: 30 min.
Resting time: 1 hr.
Rising time: 1¹/₂ hr.
Baking time: 35 min.

INGREDIENTS

¹/₂ cup fresh garlic cloves

¹/₄ cup extra-virgin olive oil

1 cup water

1 oz. fresh yeast or 1¹/₂ teaspoons
    active dry yeast

¹/₂ cup white sourdough starter
    (see page 20)

2 cups bread flour

1¹/₂ cups whole-wheat flour

2 teaspoons salt

Additional flour for assorted tasks

Special Tools

Ceramic cup or a heat-resistant
    container

Serve this bread with a small dip bowl of 2 teaspoons olive oil and ¹/₂ teaspoon balsamic vinegar.

PREPARATION

1. Place the garlic in a small saucepan and cover with the oil. Cover and cook over low heat for 45 minutes.

2. Check if tender. If not, cook for an additional 10 minutes. Remove from the heat and allow it to cool completely.

3. In the bowl of a standing electric mixer with the dough hook attached, mix the water, yeast, white sourdough starter and flours at low speed for 3 minutes. With the machine running, add the salt, switch to medium speed and continue kneading for an additional 7 minutes.

4. Place the dough in a medium greased bowl, cover with a kitchen towel and let rest until the dough has doubled in size. Check the dough after 1 hour.

5. Place the dough on a floured work surface. Using the palms of the hands, flatten the dough to form an 8 x 10-inch rectangle.

6. Spread the garlic on the rectangle and then fold dough in half to form a 5 x 8-inch rectangle.

7. Place the dough on a baking sheet lined with parchment paper. Let rise in a warm place for until the dough has doubled in size, about 1¹/₂ hours.

8. Preheat oven to 425°F. Once the dough has risen, transfer the baking sheet to the preheated oven.

9. Pour water in a ceramic cup or in a heat-resistant container and place it inside the oven to generate steam throughout the baking process.

10. Bake at 425°F for 10 minutes. Then reduce heat to 400°F and bake for an additional 25 minutes.

11. Remove from oven. Allow to cool on a wire rack for 30 minutes before serving.

WHOLE-WHEAT DRIED FRUIT BREAD

MAKES 1 LOAF

Preparation time: 30 min.
Resting time: 1 hr.
Rising time: 1 1/2 hr.
Baking time: 45 min.

INGREDIENTS

1 cup water
1/4 cup milk
1 oz. fresh yeast or 1 1/2 teaspoons
   active dry yeast
1/3 cup white sourdough starter (see p.20)
2 cups whole-wheat flour
1 1/2 cups bread flour
2 teaspoons salt
1/3 cup golden raisins
1/2 cup raisins
1/3 cup dried blueberries
1/3 cup dried cranberries
1/3 cup dried apricots
1/3 cup prunes, pitted
1 tablespoon extra-virgin olive oil,
   for greasing the bowl

Additional flour for assorted tasks

Special Tools
Nonstick 5 x 9-inch loaf pan
Ceramic cup or a heat-resistant container

This recipe takes "sweet bread" to a whole new level. In my house, I love to make sandwiches from it for my family. Each bite has a surprising taste!

PREPARATION

1. In the bowl of a standing electric mixer with the dough hook attached, mix the water, milk, yeast, white sourdough starter and flours at low speed for 3 minutes. With the machine running, add the salt, switch to medium speed and continue kneading for an additional 6 minutes.

2. Stop the machine. Add the raisins, blueberries, cranberries, apricots and prunes and knead at low speed for 2 minutes, until well blended.

3. Grease a medium bowl with the olive oil. Place the dough in the bowl, cover with kitchen towel and let rest until the dough has doubled in size. Check the dough after 1 hour.

4. Transfer the dough to a floured work surface. Place the palms of the hands on the ball and roll it backward and forward to form a cylinder, 10 inches long.

5. Place the dough in the loaf pan and flatten it out with the palm of the hand until it fits snugly.

6. Cover with kitchen towel and let rise in a warm until the dough has doubled in size, about 1 1/2 hours.

7. Preheat oven to 425°F.

8. Once the dough has risen, transfer the loaf pan into the preheated oven.

9. Pour water in a ceramic cup or in a heat-resistant container and place it inside the oven to generate steam throughout the baking process.

10. Bake 425°F for 10 minutes. Then reduce heat to 375°F and bake for an additional 35 minutes.

11. Remove from oven. Allow to cool on a wire rack for 30 minutes before serving.

DELICIOUS PUMPKIN-RAISIN BREAD

MAKES 1 LOAF

Preparation time: 30 min.
Resting time: 1 hr.
Rising time: 1¹/₂ hr.
Baking time: 45 min.

INGREDIENTS

1 cup water

¹/₄ cup milk

1 oz. fresh yeast or 1¹/₂ teaspoons
 active dry yeast

¹/₃ cup white sourdough starter (see p.20)

1 cup whole-wheat flour

1 cup rye flour

1¹/₂ cups bread flour

2 teaspoons salt

¹/₂ cup raisins

1 cup fresh pumpkin, shredded

1 tablespoon extra-virgin olive oil,
 for greasing the bowl

Additional flour for assorted tasks

Special Tools
Nonstick 5 x 9-inch loaf pan
Ceramic cup or a heat-resistant container

This bread is soft and sumptuous. It is a treat for a casual breakfast of soft-boiled eggs or for Sunday brunch. I also like to slice it and serve with a dish of roast beef or slow-cooked meat stews.

PREPARATION

1. In the bowl of a standing electric mixer with the dough hook attached, mix the water, milk, yeast, white sourdough starter and flours at low speed for 3 minutes. With the machine running, add the salt, switch to medium speed and continue kneading for an additional 6 minutes.

2. Stop the machine. Add the raisins and pumpkin and knead at low speed for 2 minutes, until well blended.

3. Grease a medium bowl with the olive oil. Place the dough in the bowl, cover with kitchen towel and let rest until the dough has doubled in size. Check the dough after 1 hour.

4. Transfer the dough to a floured work surface. Place the palms of the hands on the dough and roll it backward and forward to form a cylinder, 10 inches long.

5. Place the dough in the loaf pan and flatten it out with the palm of the hand until it fits snugly. Cover with kitchen towel and let rise in a warm place until the dough has doubled in size, about 1¹/₂ hours.

6. Preheat oven to 425°F. Once the dough has risen, use a sharp knife to make 2 diagonal slashes from the right side and 2 diagonal slashes from the left side, creating a diamond-like shape on top.

7. Transfer the loaf pan into the preheated oven. Pour water in a ceramic cup or in a heat-resistant container and place it inside the oven to generate steam throughout the baking process.

8. Bake at 425°F for 10 minutes. Then reduce heat to 375°F and bake for an additional 35 minutes.

9. Remove from oven. Allow to cool on a wire rack for 30 minutes before serving.

¤ *Delicious Pumpkin-Raisin Bread*

HEALTHY
CAKES

I PERFORMED A NUMBER OF TRIALS IN DESIGNING THESE RECIPES BEFORE I FOUND THE PERFECT COMBINATION OF INGREDIENTS. THEY NOW INCLUDE JUST THE RIGHT BALANCE OF GOOD FLAVOR AND HEALTH. THEY CALL FOR CANE SUGAR, HONEY AND WHOLE AND RYE FLOURS.

HAVE A SLICE YOURSELF OR SURPRISE YOUR LOVED ONES. SERVE THESE CAKES ON SPECIAL DISHES NEXT TO AROMATIC TEAS OR HIGH-QUALITY COFFEE. ENJOY EVERY BITE, KNOWING IT CONTAINS THE FINEST, FRESHEST INGREDIENTS. FOR THOSE OF US WITH A SWEET TOOTH, THE DOSAGE IS THE SECRET!

FOR MORE INFORMATION ABOUT WHY I CHOOSE TO USE CANE SUGAR, PLEASE SEE PAGE 17.

DELICIOUS WHOLE-WHEAT CARROT MUFFINS

MAKES 12 MUFFINS

Preparation time: 20 min.
Baking time: 20 min.

INGREDIENTS

4 eggs
3/4 cup grape seed or canola oil
1 teaspoon vanilla extract
3/4 cup cane sugar or brown sugar
1 1/4 cups whole-wheat flour
2 teaspoons baking powder
1 teaspoon ground cinnamon
1 teaspoon ground nutmeg
1/4 teaspoon salt
1 cup carrots, finely shredded
1 tablespoon butter, for greasing
   the pan

Special Tools
12-cup muffin pan

This is a healthy version of a classic carrot cake recipe. The aromatic nutmeg makes this an unforgettably delicious recipe!

PREPARATION

1. Preheat oven to 350°F.

2. Place eggs in the bowl of a standing electric mixer and beat on high speed, until fluffy.

3. With the machine running, slowly drizzle in the oil and vanilla. Continue beating until it is all incorporated. Gradually add sugar and beat until sugar is dissolved.

4. Switch to low speed and gradually add whole-wheat flour, baking powder, cinnamon, nutmeg and salt. Mix until well blended.

5. Stir in carrots.

6. Grease a muffin pan with the butter. Spoon the batter into the pan, filling each cup only 3/4 full to ensure batter doesn't spill over during baking.

7. Bake for 20 minutes or until a toothpick, inserted in the center of the cake, comes out clean.

8. Remove from oven and allow to cool completely.

✱ The muffins can be stored in an airtight container at room temperature for up to 2 days.

GRANOLA LOAF

MAKES 1 LOAF

Preparation time: 20 min.
Baking time: 45–50 min.

INGREDIENTS

4 eggs
$3/4$ cup grape seed or canola oil
1 teaspoon vanilla extract
$3/4$ cup cane sugar or brown sugar
1 cup whole-wheat flour
2 teaspoons baking powder
1 cup rolled oats
$1/3$ cup almonds, chopped
$1/2$ cup raisins
$1/4$ cup dried cranberries
1 tablespoon butter, for greasing
  the pan

Special Tools
Nonstick 5 x 9-inch loaf pan

This recipe brings together all sorts of goodness and health benefits in one cake. The oats add a rich flavor and texture. The cranberries are full of antioxidants and may improve cholesterol levels. Besides, it's also hearty and delicious. Can you ask for anything more?

PREPARATION

1. Preheat oven to 350°F.

2. Place eggs in the bowl of a standing electric mixer and beat on high speed until fluffy.

3. With the machine running, slowly drizzle in the oil and vanilla. Continue beating until it is all incorporated. Gradually add sugar and beat until sugar is dissolved.

4. Switch to low speed and gradually add whole-wheat flour and baking powder and mix until well blended.

5. Stir in rolled oats, almonds, raisins and cranberries.

6. Grease a loaf pan with the butter and pour batter into the greased pan.

7. Bake for 45-50 minutes or until a toothpick, inserted in the center of the cake, comes out clean.

8. Remove from oven and allow to cool completely.

✳ The cake can be stored in an airtight container at room temperature for up to 2 days.

¤ *Granola Loaf*

PIZZA WITH GREEN APPLE & EMMENTAL SWISS CHEESE

MAKES 3 PIZZAS

Preparation time: 20 min.
Chilling time: 2 hr.
Baking time: 4–5 min.

INGREDIENTS

Pizza dough

1^1/$_3$ cups water
1 oz. fresh yeast or 1^1/$_2$ teaspoons
  active dry yeast
3^1/$_2$ cups organic white flour
2 teaspoons salt
2 tablespoons extra-virgin olive oil

Topping

2 tablespoons butter
3 tablespoons cane sugar or
  brown sugar
4 Granny Smith apples, peeled,
  cored and cut into thin slices
9 oz. Emmental cheese, cut into
  thin slices

PREPARATION

1. In the bowl of a standing electric mixer with the dough hook attached, mix the water, yeast and flour at low speed for 3 minutes. With the machine running, add the salt, switch to medium speed and continue kneading for an additional 7 minutes.

2. On a floured surface, brush the dough with 1 tablespoon of olive oil and roll the dough into a ball.

3. Transfer the dough in a medium greased bowl and cover with plastic wrap. Let rest for 2 hours in the refrigerator.

4. Meanwhile, prepare the topping: Melt butter in a large saucepan over medium heat. Add sugar and stir until dissolved.

5. Add apples to saucepan and stir gently so the apples do not break. Reduce heat to low. Cook apples until almost tender.

6. Place a pizza stone on the bottom rack of the oven and preheat to 450°F.

7. Using a dough scraper or a knife, divide the dough into 3 equal pieces. Form each piece of dough into a ball.

8. Using a lightly floured rolling pin, roll each ball of dough on a floured surface into a very thin circle, 10 inches in diameter. Carefully transfer dough to a floured pizza paddle.

9. Place 1^1/$_2$ oz. Emmental cheese on each circle. Arrange cooked apples on top, starting at the edges and overlapping in a fan-like manner, finishing in the center. Top again with 1^1/$_2$ oz. Emmental cheese.

10. Use the pizza paddle to carefully slip one pizza onto the stone and bake for 4-5 minutes, until crust edges are golden brown. Remove and bake the other pizzas.

11. Drizzle the remaining 1 tablespoon of olive oil on pizzas and serve immediately.

¤ *Pizza with Green Apple & Emmental Swiss Cheese*

WHOLE-WHEAT DRIED FRUIT CAKE

MAKES 1 CAKE

Preparation time: 20 min.
Baking time: 40 min.

INGREDIENTS

4 eggs
1 cup grape seed or canola oil
$^3/_4$ cup cane sugar or brown sugar
1$^1/_4$ cups whole-wheat flour
2 teaspoons baking powder
$^1/_4$ cup golden raisins
$^1/_2$ cup raisins
$^1/_4$ cup dried cranberries
$^1/_4$ cup dried blueberries
1 tablespoon butter, for greasing
    the pan

Special Tools
Nonstick 5 x 9-inch loaf pan

This cake reminds me of a traditional Christmas fruitcake, but without the alcohol. No need for it, as this recipe still brings you that warm family feeling.

PREPARATION

1. Preheat oven to 375°F.

2. Place eggs in the bowl of a standing electric mixer and beat on high speed, until fluffy.

3. With the machine running, slowly drizzle in the oil and continue beating until it is all incorporated. Gradually add sugar and beat until sugar is dissolved.

4. Switch to low speed and gradually add whole-wheat flour and baking powder and mix until well blended.

5. Stir in raisins, cranberries and dried blueberries.

6. Grease a loaf pan with the butter and pour batter into the greased pan.

7. Bake for 40 minutes or until a toothpick, inserted in the center of the cake, comes out clean.

8. Remove from oven and allow to cool completely.

✱ The cake can be stored in an airtight container at room temperature for up to 2 days.

NATURAL WHOLE-WHEAT DATE CAKE

MAKES 1 CAKE

Preparation time: 20 min.
Baking time: 40–45 min.

INGREDIENTS

4 eggs

1 cup grape seed or canola oil

3/4 cup cane sugar or brown sugar

1 1/3 cups whole-wheat flour

2 teaspoons baking powder

1 1/2 cups dates, pitted and
   cut into 1/4-inch slices

1 tablespoon butter, for greasing
   the pan

Special Tools
Nonstick 5 x 9-inch loaf pan

Dates are a common ingredient in the Mediterranean basin. They are fat free, a good source of dietary fiber and contain minerals including calcium and potassium. Even after baking, they keep their special flavor.

PREPARATION

1. Preheat oven to 375°F.

2. Place eggs in the bowl of an electric mixer and beat on high speed until fluffy. With the machine running, slowly drizzle in the oil and continue beating until it is all incorporated. Gradually add sugar and beat until sugar is dissolved.

3. Switch to low speed, gradually add whole-wheat flour and baking powder and mix until well blended.

4. Stir in dates.

5. Grease a loaf pan with the butter and pour batter into the greased pan.

6. Bake for 40-45 minutes, or until a toothpick, inserted in the center of the cake, comes out clean.

7. Remove from oven and allow to cool completely.

✳ The cake can be stored in an airtight container at room temperature for up to 2 days.

ELEGANT PEAR & BROWN SUGAR PASTRY TOPPED WITH PEAR FAN

Preparation time: 20 min.
Rising time: 90 min.
Baking time: 24–27 min.

INGREDIENTS

Danish-Style Cheese Pocket and
   Cherry Pastry Dough (see page 56)
6 pears, peeled
$1/2$ cup water
$1/2$ cup cane sugar or brown sugar
$1/2$ teaspoon vanilla extract

Almond filling
$1/4$ cup softened butter
$1/2$ cup ground almonds
$1/4$ cup honey
1 egg, beaten

PREPARATION

1. Prepare the dough (for instructions see page 56). Set aside in the refrigerator.

2. In a medium saucepan, bring the pears, water and sugar to a boil over medium heat. Then lower the heat, add vanilla extract and cook for an additional 3 minutes. Remove from heat. Drain off juice and reserve. Set aside to cool.

3. Prepare the filling: Place softened butter, ground almonds, honey and egg in a small bowl. Using a rubber spatula, mix well until mixture is uniform. Set aside for later use.

4. Place the dough on a floured work surface. Using a lightly floured rolling pin, roll the dough into a 10 x 15-inch rectangle $1/8$-inch thick. Using a sharp knife, cut the dough into six 5-inch squares.

5. Using a sharp knife, make an "L"-shaped slash on the left side of each square, $1/2$ inch from the edge.

(continued on page 148)

(continued from page 147)

6. On the right side of each square, $1/2$ inch from the edge, make an upside-down "L"-shaped slash. Make sure that the top-left corner and the lower-right corner remain untouched.

7. Carefully pick up the right strip and fold it diagonally over to the left side. Carefully pick up the left strip and fold it diagonally over to the right side. Press gently to affix. The desired shape should look like a diamond with raised edges.

8. Spoon a tablespoon of the almond filling into each of the pastries.

9. Cut the pear into thin slices, taking care not to separate the slices at the stem-side, to create a fan. Place on top of filling.

10. Arrange the pastries 1-inch apart on a baking sheet lined with parchment paper.

11. Let rise in a warm place until the dough has tripled in size, about $1^{1}/_{2}$ hours.

12. Preheat the oven to 375°F 30 minutes before the end of the rising time.

13. Bake for 24-27 minutes, or until golden around the edges.

14. When thoroughly baked, remove from oven, place on wire rack and immediately brush with the pear syrup (prepared in Step 2). Let cool for 20 minutes.

15. Serve immediately or up to 5-6 hours after preparation.

＊ The pastries can be stored in an airtight container at room temperature for up to 2 days.

What a sensational presentation!
If you want to surprise your guests on special occasions with a fancy and elegant offering, this is the right pastry for you!

HAPPY HONEY RYE CAKE

MAKES 1 CAKE

Preparation time: 20 min.
Baking time: 40 min.

INGREDIENTS

4 eggs
1 cup grape seed or canola oil
3/4 cup honey
1/2 cup whole-wheat flour
1 cup whole rye flour
2 teaspoons baking powder
1 tablespoon ground cinnamon
1 tablespoon butter, for greasing
    the pan

Special Tools
Nonstick 5 x 9-inch loaf pan

I love honey cakes. During my experiments, I discovered that using rye flour creates a special and delicious version!

PREPARATION

1. Preheat oven to 375°F.

2. Place eggs in the bowl of a standing electric mixer and beat on high speed until soft and fluffy.

3. With the machine running, slowly drizzle in the oil and continue beating, until it is all incorporated. Gradually add honey and beat until blended.

4. Switch to low speed and gradually add flours, baking powder and cinnamon, mix until well blended.

5. Grease a loaf pan with the butter and pour batter into the greased pan.

6. Bake for 40 minutes or until a toothpick, inserted in the center of the cake, comes out clean.

7. Remove from oven and allow to cool completely.

✳ The cake can be stored in an airtight container at room temperature for up to 2 days.

BAKED SNACKS WITH CRANBERRIES & OATS

If you're into healthy snack bars, this one is for you. Cranberries are an amazing fruit. They possess a variety of beneficial vitamins and minerals as well as a high amount of antioxidants.

PREPARATION

1. In the bowl of a standing electric mixer with the dough hook attached, mix the water, yeast, dark sourdough starter, honey, flours and rolled oats at low speed for 3 minutes. With the machine running, add salt, switch to medium speed and continue kneading for an additional 6 minutes.

2. Stop the machine. Add cranberries and knead at low speed for 1 minute, until evenly distributed.

3. Grease a medium bowl with the butter. Place the dough in the bowl, cover with plastic wrap or a large plastic bag and let rest until the dough has doubled in size. Check the dough after about $1^1/_2$-2 hours.

4. Place the dough on a floured work surface. Using a lightly floured rolling pin, roll the dough into a 6 x 12-inch rectangle.

5. Using a sharp knife, cut the dough into strips, 4 inches long and 1 inch wide.

6. Arrange the slices $^1/_2$-inch apart on a baking sheet lined with parchment paper.

7. Let rise in a warm place until the dough has doubled in size, about $1^1/_2$ hours.

8. Preheat oven to 375°F.

9. Bake for 20 minutes, or until outside is crispy dark brown, but soft as a roll on the inside.

10. Remove from oven and allow to cool completely.

✱ The snack bars can be stored in an airtight container at room temperature for up to 2 days.

MAKES 18 SNACKS

Preparation time: 20 min.
Resting time: $1^1/_2$–2 hr.
Rising time: $1^1/_2$ hr.
Baking time: 20 min.

INGREDIENTS

$1^1/_3$ cups water
1 teaspoon active dry yeast
$^1/_3$ cup dark sourdough starter
   (see page 19)
1 tablespoon honey
1 cup whole-wheat flour
1 cup whole rye flour
$^1/_2$ cup rolled oats
1 teaspoon salt
1 cup dried cranberries
1 tablespoon softened butter,
   for greasing the bowl

DECADENT DARK CHOCOLATE LOAF

MAKES 1 LOAF

Preparation time: 20 min.
Chilling time: 30 min.
Baking time: 40–45 min.

INGREDIENTS

1/2 cup heavy whipping cream
12 oz. high-quality dark chocolate, minimum 60% cocoa, coarsely chopped
4 eggs
1/2 cup grape seed or canola oil
1 teaspoon vanilla extract
3/4 cup cane sugar or brown sugar
3/4 cup whole-wheat flour
2 teaspoons baking powder
1/2 teaspoon salt
1/2 cup high-quality cocoa
1 tablespoon butter, for greasing the pan

Special Tools
Nonstick 5 x 9-inch loaf pan

PREPARATION

1. In a small saucepan bring whipping cream just to a boil over medium heat. Then remove from heat.

2. Add chopped chocolate. Wait about 3 minutes until chocolate melts. Using a whisk, mix cream and chocolate until the consistency is smooth and shiny. Remove from heat and allow mixture to cool slightly.

3. Tranfer mixture to a bowl. Cover and place in the refrigerator for 1 hour or until firm enough to shape.

4. In the meanwhile, place eggs in the bowl of an electric mixer and beat on high speed until fluffy. With the machine running, slowly drizzle in the oil and continue beating, until it is all incorporated. Gradually add vanilla and sugar, beat until sugar is dissolved.

5. Switch to low speed and gradually add whole-wheat flour, baking powder, salt and cocoa. Mix until well blended.

6. Remove the chilled chocolate mixture from the refrigerator. Using a tablespoon, scoop out 6 tablespoon-sized portions. With your palms, gently roll each portion into a ball.

7. Pour 1/3 of the batter into a greased loaf pan. Place the 6 chocolate balls on top and pour over the remaining batter.

8. Preheat oven to 350°F. Bake for 40-45 minutes, or until a toothpick, inserted in the center of the cake, comes out clean.

9. Remove from oven and allow to cool completely.

✱ The cake can be stored in an airtight container at room temperature for up to 2 days.

CHERRY CAKE

Cherry cake is perfect for early summer when this fruit is at its peak. Serve it on a breezy evening at a gathering and it will all be gone before you know it!

MAKES 1 CAKE

Preparation time: 20 min.
Baking time: 40–45 min.

INGREDIENTS

4 eggs
1 cup grape seed or canola oil
$3/4$ cup cane sugar or brown sugar
$1 1/3$ cups whole-wheat flour
2 teaspoons baking powder
$3/4$ pound fresh cherries, pitted
1 tablespoon butter, for greasing
   the bowl

Special Tools
Nonstick 5 x 9-inch loaf pan

PREPARATION

1. Preheat oven to 375°F.

2. Place eggs in the bowl of a standing electric mixer and beat on high speed until fluffy.

3. With the machine running, slowly drizzle in the oil and continue beating, until it is all incorporated. Gradually add sugar and beat until sugar is dissolved.

4. Switch to low speed, gradually add whole-wheat flour and baking powder and mix until well blended.

5. Stir in cherries.

6. Grease a loaf pan with the butter and pour batter into the greased pan.

7. Bake for 40-45 minutes, or until a toothpick, inserted in the center of the cake, comes out clean.

8. Remove from oven and allow to cool completely.

✳ The cake can be stored in an airtight container at room temperature for up to 2 days.

SUMMERY APRICOT CAKE

MAKES 1 CAKE

Preparation time: 20 min.
Baking time: 40–45 min.

INGREDIENTS

³/₄ pound fresh apricots, cut
   into quarters
2 tablespoons honey
1 tablespoon premium rum
4 eggs
1 cup grape seed or canola oil
³/₄ cup cane sugar or brown sugar
1¹/₃ cups whole-wheat flour
2 teaspoons baking powder
1 tablespoon butter, for greasing
   the pan

Special Tools
Nonstick 5 x 9-inch loaf pan

Fresh apricots—one of the first signs of summer. They are full of beta-carotene, important for a healthy heart and offer a plentiful supply of vitamin C. All of this and more make this slightly tart cake an absolute treat alongside an afternoon cup of tea.

PREPARATION

1. Combine apricots, honey and rum in a small bowl. Set aside for later use.

2. Preheat oven to 375°F.

3. Place eggs in the bowl of a standing electric mixer and beat on high speed until fluffy.

4. With the machine running, slowly drizzle in the oil and continue beating, until it is all incorporated. Gradually add sugar and beat until sugar is dissolved.

5. Switch to low speed, gradually add whole-wheat flour and baking powder and mix until well blended.

6. Stir in apricot mixture.

7. Grease a loaf pan with the butter and pour batter into the greased pan.

8. Bake for 40-45 minutes, or until a toothpick, inserted in the center of the cake, comes out clean.

9. Remove from oven and allow to cool completely.

✱ The cake can be stored in an airtight container at room temperature for up to 2 days.

EXOTIC PUMPKIN MARSALA MINI-CAKES

MAKES 12 CAKES

Preparation time: 20 min.
Baking time: 30–35 min.

INGREDIENTS

4 eggs

³/₄ cup grape seed or canola oil

³/₄ cup cane sugar or brown sugar

1¹/₄ cups whole-wheat flour

2 teaspoons baking powder

¹/₂ teaspoon ground cloves

¹/₂ teaspoon ground nutmeg

¹/₂ teaspoon ground anise seeds

2 cups fresh pumpkin, peeled and
   finely shredded

3 tablespoons Marsala wine

1 tablespoon butter, for greasing
   the muffin pan

Special Tools

12-cup muffin pan

You can add pumpkin to a variety of recipes. The delightful combination of pumpkin and Marsala wine has a distinctive flavor and is very rich. This recipe can be also used to make a loaf cake instead of mini-cakes. Just pour the batter into a 5 x 9-inch loaf pan (see similar instructions on page 155).

PREPARATION

1. Preheat oven to 350°F.

2. Place eggs in the bowl of a standing electric mixer and beat on high speed until fluffy.

3. With the machine running, slowly drizzle in the oil and continue beating, until it is all incorporated. Gradually add sugar and beat until sugar is dissolved.

4. Switch to low speed, gradually add whole-wheat flour, baking powder, ground cloves, nutmeg and anise seeds and mix until well blended.

5. Stir in pumpkin and Marsala wine.

6. Grease a muffin pan with the butter. Spoon the batter into the pan, filling each cup only ³/₄ full to ensure batter doesn't spill over during baking.

7. Bake for 30-35 minutes, or until a toothpick, inserted in the center of the cake, comes out clean.

8. Remove from oven and allow to cool completely.

✱ The mini-cakes can be stored in an airtight container at room temperature for up to 2 days.

¤ *Exotic Pumpkin Marsala Mini-Cakes*

ORANGE KUGELHOPF CAKE

MAKES 1 CAKE

Preparation time: 1 hr.
Chilling time: 1 hr.
Baking time: 55–60 min.

INGREDIENTS

$1/2$ cup cane sugar or brown sugar
2 tablespoons water
2 fresh oranges, sliced, with peel
4 eggs
1 cup grape seed or canola oil
1 teaspoon vanilla extract
$2/3$ cup cane sugar or brown sugar
$1 1/2$ cups whole-wheat flour
2 teaspoons baking powder
$1/2$ teaspoon salt
1 tablespoon butter, for greasing
   the pan

Special Tools
8-inch Kugelhopf mold or small
   tube pan

After many attempts, I can honestly say this is the best orange cake I have ever made! For a milder orange flavor, use the orange zest for syrup and discard remainder of peel.

PREPARATION

1. In a medium saucepan, heat $1/2$ cup sugar with the water over medium heat, until the sugar starts to bubble. Then reduce the heat and add the oranges. Cook for 40 minutes. Remove from heat and cool for 20 minutes.

2. Pour the orange mixture into a food processor fitted with a metal blade. Process until mixture is smooth.

3. Preheat oven to 325°F.

4. Place eggs in the bowl of a standing electric mixer and beat on high speed until fluffy. With the machine running, slowly drizzle in the oil and continue beating until it is all incorporated. Gradually add vanilla and sugar and beat until sugar is dissolved.

5. Switch to low speed, gradually add whole-wheat flour, baking powder and salt, mix until well blended.

6. Stir in the orange mixture (prepared in Step 2).

7. Grease pan with the butter and pour batter into the greased pan.

8. Bake for 55-60 minutes, or until a toothpick, inserted in the center of the cake, comes out clean.

9. Remove from oven and allow to cool completely.

✳ The cake can be stored in an airtight container at room temperature for up to 2 days.

¤ *Orange Kugelhopf Cake*

POWER
COOKIES

TO ME, COOKIES ARE DELIGHTFUL AND FUN TO HAVE AT HOME. THEY ARE A GREAT TREAT FOR GUESTS OR TO ENJOY BY YOURSELF WITH A HOT CUP OF COFFEE OR TEA. IN THE AFTERNOON, WHEN THE KIDS LOOK FOR SOMETHING TO SATISFY THEIR SWEET TOOTH, A JAR OF HOMEMADE COOKIES WILL ALWAYS SUCCEED IN CONQUERING THEIR CRAVINGS.

IT IS ALSO A GREAT OPPORTUNITY FOR SOME QUALITY TIME WITH CHILDREN. KIDS LOVE TO PARTICIPATE IN THE COOKIE-MAKING PROCESS. AT THE SAME TIME, YOU CAN ALSO TEACH THEM HOW TO: FOLLOW A RECIPE, SHOW THEM BASIC CLEANING SKILLS AND, ABOVE ALL, ENJOY CREATING SOMETHING AS A FAMILY!

THERE ARE THOUSANDS OF RECIPES FOR COOKIES, BUT THE ONES IN THIS BOOK ARE FUN AND EASY TO PREPARE IN YOUR HOME KITCHEN. MOREOVER, THESE COOKIES ARE FULL OF A VARIETY OF NUTRIENTS AND TASTY INGREDIENTS!

IN THESE RECIPES YOU CAN CONVERT THE $3/4$ CUP OF BUTTER TO $1/3$ CUP OF BUTTER AT ROOM TEMPERATURE PLUS $1/3$ CUP GRAPE SEED OIL. FOR MORE INFORMATION ABOUT WHY I CHOOSE TO USE BUTTER AND CANE SUGAR, SEE PAGES 16-17.

SAVORY CHEESE COOKIES

In my home these cookies are a must-have in the pantry. Once you taste them, you will be hooked and just won't be able to stop munching on them. Both an appetizer and a snack, they are perfect to serve at brunch or as part of a light meal for the kids next to colorful, eye-catching vegetables.

MAKES 30 COOKIES

Preparation time: 20 min.
Chilling time: 30 min.
Baking time: 8–10 min.

INGREDIENTS

3/4 cup butter, room temperature
1 egg
1 tablespoon water
1/2 teaspoon salt
2 cups whole-wheat flour
1/2 teaspoon baking powder
1/4 cup Emmental cheese, finely
    shredded
2 tablespoons Parmesan cheese,
    grated

PREPARATION

1. Cream butter in the bowl of a standing electric mixer, beating with the mixer's flat beater on low speed for 3 minutes until smooth.

2. Add egg, water, salt, flour and baking powder, continuing to mix on low speed for 2 minutes.

3. Add Emmental and Parmesan cheeses and mix for an additional 2 minutes until well distributed.

4. Cover with plastic wrap and place in the refrigerator for 30 minutes.

5. Preheat oven to 375°F.

6. Transfer the dough to a floured work surface. Using your hands, shape the dough into a cylinder, about 1-inch in diameter. Using a sharp knife, cut the roll into slices, 1/2-inch thick.

7. Arrange the slices 1/2-inch apart on a baking sheet lined with parchment paper.

8. Bake for 8-10 minutes or until golden brown.

9. Remove from oven. Allow to cool completely on a wire rack for 15-20 minutes and serve.

✱ Store cookies in an airtight container at room temperature for up to a week.

FRUITY GRANOLA ENERGY COOKIES

MAKES 20 COOKIES

Preparation time: 20 min.
Chilling time: 30 min.
Baking time: 15–17 min.

INGREDIENTS

³/₄ cup butter, room temperature
¹/₂ cup honey
2 eggs
1 teaspoon vanilla extract
2 tablespoons brandy
¹/₂ teaspoon salt
1 cup whole-wheat flour
2 teaspoons baking powder
2¹/₄ cups rolled oats
¹/₂ cup dried blueberries
1 beaten egg, for brushing

Special Tools
Two 12-cup muffin pans

PREPARATION

1. Cream butter and honey in the bowl of a standing electric mixer, beating with the mixer's flat beater on low speed for 3 minutes or until mixture is smooth.

2. Add eggs, vanilla extract, brandy, salt, whole-wheat flour and baking powder, continuing to mix on low speed for 2 minutes.

3. Add rolled oats and blueberries and mix for an additional 2 minutes, until mixture is uniform.

4. Cover with plastic wrap and place in the refrigerator for 30 minutes.

5. Preheat oven to 375°F.

6. Grease each of the muffin pans.

7. Spoon 2 tablespoons of the batter into each cup. Level off the top to make it flat instead of domed, and brush with beaten egg. Repeat process with the remaining batter.

8. Bake for 15-17 minutes or until golden brown.

9. Remove from oven. Allow to cool completely on a wire rack for 15-20 minutes and serve.

✳ Store cookies in an airtight container at room temperature for up to a week.

¤ *Rich Granola & Dark Chocolate Cookies*

RICH GRANOLA & DARK CHOCOLATE COOKIES

MAKES 60 COOKIES

Preparation time: 20 min.
Chilling time: 2 hr.
Baking time: 10–12 min.

INGREDIENTS

$3/4$ cup butter, room temperature
$1/2$ cup cane sugar or brown sugar
2 eggs
1 teaspoon vanilla extract
2 tablespoons brandy
$1/2$ teaspoon salt
1 cup whole-wheat flour
1 teaspoon baking powder
1 cup rolled oats
$1/3$ cup dark chocolate chips
$1/4$ cup sliced almonds
1 beaten egg, for brushing

These cookies are for people who love the taste of dark chocolate. They have a crunchy texture and subtle sweetness.

PREPARATION

1. Cream butter and sugar in the bowl of a standing electric mixer, beating with the mixer's flat beater on low speed for 3 minutes or until mixture is smooth.

2. Add eggs, vanilla extract, brandy, salt, whole-wheat flour and baking powder, continuing to mix on low speed for 2 minutes.

3. Add rolled oats, chocolate chips and sliced almonds and mix for an additional 2 minutes, until mixture is uniform.

4. Cover with plastic wrap and place in the refrigerator for 2 hours.

5. Preheat oven to 375°F.

6. Transfer the dough to a floured work surface. Using your hands, shape the dough into a cylinder, about 2 inches in diameter.

7. Use both hands to press the cylinder down into a rectangle, 2-inch wide by 1-inch thick.

8. Using a sharp knife, cut the roll into slices $1/4$-inch thick. (Each slice should be approximately 2 x 1-inch and $1/4$-inch wide).

9. Arrange the slices $1/2$-inch apart on a baking sheet lined with parchment paper and brush the slices with the beaten egg.

10. Bake for 10-12 minutes or until golden brown.

11. Remove from oven. Allow to cool completely on a wire rack for 15-20 minutes and serve.

✳ Store cookies in an airtight container at room temperature for up to a week.

WHOLE-WHEAT CHOCOLATE COOKIES

These cookies are tasty and perfect for the moment when you feel the urge for a sweet treat. I prepare these with dark chocolate because it is healthier and adds a richer flavor. Milk chocolate may be substituted as well.

MAKES 40 COOKIES

Preparation time: 20 min.
Chilling time: 30 min.
Baking time: 12–14 min.

INGREDIENTS

3/4 cup butter, room temperature
1/2 cup cane sugar or brown sugar
1 egg
1 teaspoon vanilla extract
1 tablespoon water
1/2 teaspoon salt
1 cup whole-wheat flour
1 cup organic white flour
1/2 teaspoon baking powder
1/2 cup premium dark chocolate,
   70% cocoa, coarsely chopped

PREPARATION

1. Cream butter and sugar in the bowl of a standing electric mixer, beating with the mixer's flat beater on low speed for 3 minutes or until mixture is smooth.

2. Add egg, vanilla extract, water, salt, flours and baking powder, continuing to mix on low speed for 2 minutes.

3. Add chopped chocolate and mix for an additional 1 minute, until well distributed.

4. Cover with plastic wrap and place in the refrigerator for 30 minutes.

5. Preheat oven to 375°F.

6. Transfer the dough to a floured work surface. Using a rolling pin, roll the dough to a thickness of about 1/4-inch.

7. Using a 2-inch round cookie cutter, cut out dough and place 1/2-inch apart on a baking sheet lined with parchment paper.

8. Bake for 12-14 minutes or until golden brown.

9. Remove from oven. Allow to cool completely on a wire rack for 15-20 minutes and serve.

✱ Store cookies in an airtight container at room temperature for up to a week.

WHOLE-WHEAT TAHINI COOKIES

MAKES 20 COOKIES

Preparation time: 20 min.
Chilling time: 30 min.
Baking time: 12—15 min.

INGREDIENTS

$1/3$ cup butter, room temperature
$1/4$ cup cane sugar or brown sugar
1 egg
$1/4$ cup tahini (sesame seed paste)
$1/2$ teaspoon salt
1 cup whole-wheat flour
$1/2$ teaspoon baking powder

The addition of tahini to your cookie dough results in a very crisp and nutty cookie. These cookies are wonderful for kids. Ask them to help you and they will certainly be tempted to take a bite.

PREPARATION

1. Cream butter and sugar in the bowl of a standing electric mixer, beating with the mixer's flat beater on low speed for 3 minutes or until mixture is smooth.

2. Add egg, tahini paste, salt, whole-wheat flour and baking powder, continuing to mix on low speed for 3 minutes.

3. Cover with plastic wrap and place in the refrigerator for 30 minutes.

4. Preheat oven to 375°F.

5. Transfer the dough to a floured work surface. Using a rolling pin, roll the dough to a thickness of about $1/4$-inch.

6. Using a 2-inch round cookie cutter, cut out dough and place $1/2$-inch apart on a baking sheet lined with parchment paper.

7. Bake for 12-15 minutes or until golden brown.

8. Remove from oven. Allow to cool completely on a wire rack for 15-20 minutes and serve.

✳ Store cookies in an airtight container at room temperature for up to a week.

CARAMEL MINI-COOKIES WITH TOASTED HAZELNUTS

This nutty cookie is based on hazelnut praline. Hazelnuts are my favorite and I include them in a variety of dishes in my kitchen. The texture of this cookie is very crisp and the nutty flavor is dominant. I love to serve them alongside a cup of coffee, as a dessert with a glass of brandy or with an aromatic liqueur.

MAKES 24 COOKIES

Preparation time: 20 min.
Baking time: 10–12 min.

INGREDIENTS

3 egg whites
$^1/_2$ cup cane sugar or brown sugar
$^1/_2$ cup roasted hazelnut praline paste
1 teaspoon amaretto liqueur
$^1/_2$ cup whole hazelnuts, toasted
   and skinned

Garnish
$^1/_4$ cup whole hazelnuts, toasted
   and skinned

PREPARATION

1. Preheat oven to 375°F.

2. Whisk egg whites on high speed in the bowl of a standing electric mixer, until light and fluffy. With the machine running, gradually add the sugar until it has all been absorbed into the eggs and stiff peaks form.

3. Remove bowl from mixer. Gently fold hazelnut paste into the egg mixture with a rubber spatula, until the mixture is smooth and uniform in color.

4. Gently fold in amaretto liqueur and $^1/_2$ cup of hazelnuts until combined.

5. Spoon 1 full tablespoon of the batter onto a baking sheet lined with parchment paper. Repeat with the remaining mixture, spacing 1-inch apart.

6. Bake for 10-12 minutes, until golden brown or cookies start to crack on top and the cookie crust hardens.

7. Remove from oven. Allow to cool completely on a wire rack for 15-20 minutes and serve.

✱ Store cookies in an airtight container at room temperature for up to a week.

BROWN SUGAR NUT COOKIES

These crusty cookies are an improved version of butter cookies, with the addition of walnuts. They are perfect to start off the morning with your cup of coffee, enjoy with afternoon tea or at the end of a lovely dinner, with some fresh fruit.

MAKES 40 COOKIES

Preparation time: 20 min.
Chilling time: 30 min.
Baking time: 8–10 min.

INGREDIENTS

$3/4$ cup butter, room temperature
$1/2$ cup cane sugar or brown sugar
2 eggs
1 teaspoon vanilla extract
$1/2$ cup walnuts, choppped
$1/2$ teaspoon salt
1 cup whole-wheat flour
1 cup organic white flour
$1/2$ teaspoon baking powder

PREPARATION

1. Cream butter and sugar in the bowl of a standing electric mixer, beating with the mixer's flat beater on low speed for 3 minutes or until mixture is smooth.

2. Add eggs, vanilla extract, walnuts, salt, flours and baking powder, continuing to mix on low speed for 3 minutes.

3. Cover with plastic wrap and place in the refrigerator for 30 minutes.

4. Preheat oven to 375°F.

5. Spoon 1 tablespoon of the batter onto a baking sheet lined with parchment paper. Repeat with the remaining mixture, spacing 1-inch apart.

6. Bake for 8-10 minutes or until golden brown.

7. Remove from oven. Allow to cool completely on a wire rack for 15-20 minutes and serve.

✱ Store cookies in an airtight container at room temperature for up to a week.

WHOLESOME HONEY SESAME COOKIES

I prepared these cookies during my first working visit to China. My goal was to expose my hosts to Western tastes. The Chinese really like sesame seeds and these cookies were a smashing success.

MAKES 30 COOKIES

Preparation time: 20 min.
Chilling time: 30 min.
Baking time: 8–10 min.

INGREDIENTS

$^3/_4$ cup butter, room temperature
$^1/_3$ cup honey
2 eggs
$^1/_3$ cup sesame seeds
$^1/_2$ teaspoon salt
2 cups whole-wheat flour
$^1/_2$ teaspoon baking powder

PREPARATION

1. Cream butter and honey in the bowl of a standing electric mixer, beating with the mixer's flat beater on low speed for 3 minutes or until mixture is smooth.

2. Add eggs, sesame seeds, salt, whole-wheat flour and baking powder, continuing to mix on low speed for 3 minutes.

3. Cover with plastic wrap and place in the refrigerator for 30 minutes.

4. Preheat oven to 375°F.

5. Transfer the dough to a floured work surface. Using a rolling pin, roll the dough to a thickness of about $^1/_4$-inch.

6. Using a 2-inch round cookie cutter, cut out dough and place $^1/_2$-inch apart on a baking sheet lined with parchment paper.

7. Bake for 8-10 minutes or until golden brown.

8. Remove from oven. Allow to cool completely on a wire rack for 15-20 minutes and serve.

✱ Store cookies in an airtight container at room temperature for up to a week.

TANGY CRANBERRY & PISTACHIO COOKIES

These cookies have a complex texture. The cranberries provide softness while the pistachio nuts add crunch. This combination creates a very interesting flavor and texture. These cookies are an excellent morning boost and can also add a spring to your step over afternoon tea or coffee.

MAKES 50 COOKIES

Preparation time: 20 min.
Chilling time: 30 min.
Baking time: 8—10 min.

INGREDIENTS

$3/4$ cup butter, room temperature
$1/4$ cup cane sugar or brown sugar
2 eggs
$1/3$ cup dried unsweetened cranberries
$1/4$ cup pistachios, coarsely chopped
$1/2$ teaspoon salt
2 cups whole-wheat flour
$1/2$ teaspoon baking powder

PREPARATION

1. Cream butter and sugar in the bowl of a standing electric mixer, beating with the mixer's flat beater on low speed for 3 minutes or until mixture is smooth.

2. Add eggs, cranberries, pistachios, salt, whole-wheat flour and baking powder, continuing to mix on low speed for 3 minutes.

3. Cover with plastic wrap and place in the refrigerator for 30 minutes.

4. Preheat oven to 375°F.

5. Transfer the dough to a floured work surface. Using a rolling pin, roll the dough to a thickness of about $1/4$-inch.

6. Using a 2-inch round or cookie cutter, cut out dough and place $1/2$-inch apart on a baking sheet lined with parchment paper.

7. Bake for 8-10 minutes or until golden brown.

8. Remove from oven. Allow to cool completely on a wire rack for 15-20 minutes and serve.

✱ Store cookies in an airtight container at room temperature for up to a week.

¤ *Tangy Cranberry & Pistachio Cookies*

ALMOND MARZIPAN COOKIES

MAKES 25 COOKIES

Preparation time: 20 min.
Chilling time: 30 min.
Baking time: 7–9 min.

INGREDIENTS

$3/4$ cup butter, room temperature
$1/4$ cup cane sugar or brown sugar
$1/4$ cup marzipan
2 eggs
1 tablespoon amaretto liqueur
$1/2$ teaspoon salt
$1 1/2$ cups whole-wheat flour
$1/2$ cup ground almonds
$1/2$ teaspoon baking powder

Garnish
Whole almonds

I love marzipan and I include it in many of the sweets that I prepare. In addition to the wonderful taste, the smell of these cookies is addictive.

PREPARATION

1. Cream butter, sugar and marzipan in the bowl of a standing electric mixer, beating with the mixer's flat beater on low speed for 3 minutes or until mixture is smooth.

2. Add eggs, amaretto liqueur, salt, whole-wheat flour, ground almonds and baking powder, continuing to mix on low speed for 3 minutes.

3. Cover with plastic wrap and place in the refrigerator for 30 minutes.

4. Preheat oven to 375°F.

5. Roll 1 tablespoon of dough into a ball.

6. Place on a baking sheet lined with parchment paper. Repeat with the remaining dough, spacing 1-inch apart.

7. Gently press a whole almond into the top of each cookie.

8. Bake for 7-9 minutes or until golden brown.

9. Remove from oven. Allow to cool completely on a wire rack for 15-20 minutes and serve.

✱ Store cookies in an airtight container at room temperature for up to a week.

¤ *Almond Marzipan Cookies*

SALTED OATMEAL COOKIES

MAKES 35 COOKIES

Preparation time: 20 min.
Chilling time: 30 min.
Baking time: 8–10 min.

INGREDIENTS

$3/4$ cup butter, room temperature
2 eggs
$1/3$ cup raw sesame seeds
$1/2$ cup rolled oats
1 teaspoon salt
2 cups whole-wheat flour
$1/2$ teaspoon baking powder

Garnish
2 tablespoons extra-virgin olive oil
1 teaspoon coarse salt

I like to serve these cookies as a dinner appetizer alongside a chilled glass of white wine.

PREPARATION

1. Cream butter in the bowl of a standing electric mixer, beating with the mixer's flat beater on low speed for 3 minutes or until butter is smooth.

2. Add eggs, sesame seeds, rolled oats, salt, whole-wheat flour and baking powder, continuing to mix on low speed for 3 minutes.

3. Cover with plastic wrap and place in the refrigerator for 30 minutes.

4. Preheat oven to 375°F.

5. Transfer the dough to a floured work surface. Using a rolling pin, roll the dough to a thickness of about $1/4$-inch.

6. Using a 2-inch round cookie cutter, cut out dough and place $1/2$-inch apart on a baking sheet lined with parchment paper.

7. Brush with olive oil and sprinkle with coarse salt.

8. Bake for 8-10 minutes or until golden brown.

9. Remove from oven. Allow to cool completely on a wire rack for 15-20 minutes and serve.

✳ Store cookies in an airtight container at room temperature for up to a week.

PECAN COOKIES

All you pecan lovers, search no more —this is the cookie for you!

MAKES 30 COOKIES

Preparation time: 20 min.
Chilling time: 30 min.
Baking time: 8—10 min.

INGREDIENTS

$3/4$ cup butter, room temperature
$1/2$ cup cane sugar or brown sugar
2 eggs
1 tablespoon brandy
$1/2$ teaspoon salt
$1 1/2$ cups whole-wheat flour
$3/4$ cup pecans, finely chopped
$1/2$ teaspoon baking powder

PREPARATION

1. Cream butter and sugar in the bowl of a standing electric mixer, beating with the mixer's flat beater on low speed for 3 minutes or until mixture is smooth.

2. Add eggs, brandy, salt, whole-wheat flour, pecans and baking powder, continuing to mix on low speed for 3 minutes.

3. Cover with plastic wrap and place in the refrigerator for 30 minutes.

4. Preheat oven to 375°F.

5. Transfer the dough to a floured work surface. Using a rolling pin, roll the dough to a thickness of about $1/4$-inch.

6. Using a 2-inch round cookie cutter, cut out dough and place $1/2$-inch apart on a baking sheet lined with parchment paper.

7. Bake for 8-10 minutes or until golden brown.

8. Remove from oven. Allow to cool completely on a wire rack for 15-20 minutes and serve.

✳ Store cookies in an airtight container at room temperature for up to a week.

DELICATE HERB CRACKER-COOKIES

MAKES 50 COOKIES

Preparation time: 20 min.
Chilling time: 30 min.
Baking time: 5–7 min.

INGREDIENTS

3/4 cup butter, room temperature
2 eggs
2 tablespoons basil, coarsely chopped
1 tablespoon oregano, finely chopped
3 tablespoons parsley, finely chopped
1 teaspoon salt
2 cups whole-wheat flour
1/2 teaspoon baking powder
1/3 cup raw sesame seeds

Garnish
2 tablespoons extra-virgin olive oil
1 teaspoon coarse salt
2 oz. Parmesan cheese, cut into
    thin slices

The addition of herbs to this dough makes these crackers perfect for a sophisticated crowd on a casual evening or a fancy cocktail party. Serve them as an appetizer with a tasty dip or on their own.

PREPARATION

1. Cream butter in the bowl of a standing electric mixer, beating with the mixer's flat beater on low speed for 3 minutes or until butter is smooth.

2. Add eggs, chopped basil, oregano, parsley, salt, whole-wheat flour, baking powder and sesame seeds, continuing to mix on low speed for 3 minutes.

3. Cover with plastic wrap and place in the refrigerator for 30 minutes.

4. Preheat oven to 375°F.

5. Transfer the dough to a floured work surface. Using a rolling pin, roll the dough to a thickness of about 1/8-inch.

6. Using a 2-inch round cookie cutter, cut out dough and place 1/2-inch apart on a baking sheet lined with parchment paper.

7. Brush with olive oil and sprinkle with a pinch of coarse salt.

8. Bake for 5-7 minutes or until golden brown.

9. Remove from oven. Allow to cool on a wire rack for 15-20 minutes and serve.

Serving option: Use a carrot peeler to slice a few slivers of Parmesan cheese. Place them on top of the cookies before serving.

✳ The cookies can be stored in an airtight container at room temperature for up to a week.

FREESTYLE HEALTH COOKIES

The kids will love to help you prepare these tasty and easy-to-make freestyle cookies. The fact that they are packed with healthy ingredients just makes them twice as rewarding for you as well! Choose your favorite granola — the one you have at home, preferably without any additives.

MAKES 50 COOKIES

Preparation time: 20 min.
Chilling time: 30 min.
Baking time: 8–10 min.

INGREDIENTS

3/4 cup butter, room temperature
1/4 cup cane sugar or brown sugar
2 eggs
1/4 cup walnuts, coarsely chopped
1/4 cup pistachios, peeled,
   coarsely chopped
1/4 cup dried cranberries
1/3 cup granola
1/2 teaspoon salt
2 cups whole-wheat flour
1/2 teaspoon baking powder

PREPARATION

1. Cream butter and sugar in the bowl of a standing electric mixer, beating with the mixer's flat beater on low speed for 3 minutes or until mixture is smooth.

2. Add eggs, walnuts, pistachios, cranberries, granola, salt, whole-wheat flour and baking powder, continuing to mix on low speed for 3 minutes.

3. Cover with plastic wrap and place in the refrigerator for 30 minutes.

4. Preheat oven to 375°F.

5. Spoon 1 tablespoon of the batter onto a baking sheet lined with parchment paper. Repeat with the remaining batter mixture, spacing each tablespoonful 1-inch apart.

6. Bake for 8-10 minutes or until golden brown.

7. Remove from oven. Allow to cool completely on a wire rack for 15-20 minutes and serve.

✽ Store cookies in an airtight container at room temperature for up to a week.

INDEX

A

Almond Marzipan Cookies, 178
Aromatic Herb Bread, 63

B

Baked Snacks with Cranberries & Oats, 150
Beet & Anise Bread, 93
Breadsticks with Tomatoes & Herbs, 44
Brown Sugar Nut Cookies, 174

C

Caramel Mini-Cookies with Toasted Hazelnuts, 173
Caramel-Pecan Buns, 50
Cherry Cake, 154
Classic Braided Shabbat Challah, 68
Classic German Rye Bread, 120
Classic Rye Bagels, 91
Country Bread with Wakame Seaweed, 126
Country Rye Bread, 70
Crunchy Sesame Bagels, 43

D

Danish-Style Cheese Pocket & Cherry Pastry, 56
Dark Classic Country Baguettes, 86
Decadent Dark Chocolate Loaf, 153
Decadent Fig & Goat Cheese Stuffed Bread, 114
Delicate Herb Cracker-Cookies, 183
Delicious Pumpkin-Raisin Bread, 134
Delicious Whole-Wheat Carrot Muffins, 139

E

Earthy Seed Loaf, 112
Eggplant & Caciotta Cheese Bread, 128
Elegant Pear & Brown Sugar Pastry Topped with Pear Fan, 147
Exotic Pumpkin Marsala Mini-Cakes, 156

F

Flavorful Mediterranean Bagels, 99
Freestyle Health Cookies, 184
French-Style Country Bread, 82
Fruity Granola Energy Cookies, 164

G

Garlic Confit Focaccia, 131
Granola Loaf, 140

H

Happy Honey Rye Cake, 149
Hazelnut Bread, 125
Healthy Focaccia, 64
Healthy-Harvest Grain Bread, 73
Healthy Whole-Wheat Carrot Pastry, 59
Hearty Rye Bread with Dried Fruit, 85
Honey-Lemon Bread, 123

I

Indulgent Dark Chocolate Sourdough Bread, 77
Italian Walnut Bread, 109

L

Long & Twisted Whole-Grain Breadsticks, 36

M

Mediterranean Sesame-Coated Bread, 88
Milk & Honey Mini-Rolls, 32

N

Natural Whole-Wheat Date Cake, 145

O

Orange Kugelhopf Cake, 158

P

Parmesan Rolls, 84
Pecan Cookies, 181
Pistachio & Brown Sugar Feast, 53
Pizza with Green Apple & Emmental Swiss Cheese, 142
Prune & Port Whole-Wheat Bread, 118

R

Rich Granola & Dark Chocolate Cookies, 167
Rich Olive Bread, 100
Rye & Olive Breadsticks, 31
Rye Breadsticks with Cheese, 48

S

Salted Oatmeal Cookies, 180
Savory Breadsticks, 34
Savory Cheese Cookies, 163
Savory Whole-Grain Pastry, 46
Seeded Classic Ciabatta, 102
Special Whole-Grain Rolls, 49
Spiced Breadsticks with Poppy Seeds, 40
Spiced Cheese & Nut Bread, 117
Summery Apricot Cake, 155
Sweet Anise-Scented Baguettes, 94
Sweet Chili & Cilantro Bread, 104

T

Tangy Cranberry & Pistachio Cookies, 176
Three-Color Sesame Rolls, 105
Two-Color Herb Bread, 75

U

Unique Wintry Chestnut Bread, 122

W

Whole-Grain Carrot Bread, 110
Wholesome Honey Sesame Cookies, 175
Whole-Wheat Bread with Flax Seeds, 71
Whole-Wheat Chocolate Cookies, 168
Whole-Wheat Dried Fruit Bread, 132
Whole-Wheat Dried Fruit Cake, 144
Whole-Wheat Tahini Cookies, 170
Worker's Dark Bread, 81

Y

Yellow Cheese & Wild Mushroom Bread, 115

Z

Zesty Roasted Corn & Chili Bread—Ciabatta Style, 96

CONVERSION CHARTS

Standard United States measures are used for the recipes in this cookbook. The information presented in the following Conversion Charts can be used to determine *approximate* metric equivalents.

METRIC EQUIVALENTS
FOR DIFFERENT TYPES OF INGREDIENTS

A standard cup measure of a dry or solid ingredient will vary in weight depending on the type of ingredient. A standard cup of liquid is the same volume for any type of liquid. Use the following chart when converting standard cup measures to grams (weight) or milliliters (volume).

Standard Cup		Fine Powder (ex. flour)		Grain (ex.rice)		Granular (ex. sugar)		Liquid Solids (ex. butter)		Liquid (ex. milk)
1	=	140 g	=	150 g	=	190 g	=	200 g	=	240 ml
3/4	=	105 g	=	113 g	=	143 g	=	150 g	=	180 ml
2/3	=	93 g	=	100 g	=	125 g	=	133 g	=	160 ml
1/2	=	70 g	=	75 g	=	95 g	=	100 g	=	120 ml
1/3	=	47 g	=	50 g	=	63 g	=	67 g	=	80 ml
1/4	=	35 g	=	38 g	=	48 g	=	50 g	=	60 ml
1/8	=	18 g	=	19 g	=	24 g	=	25 g	=	30 ml

USEFUL EQUIVALENTS FOR DRY INGREDIENTS BY WEIGHT

To convert ounces to grams, multiply the number of oz by 30

1 oz	=	$^1/_{16}$ lb	=	30g
4 oz	=	$^1/_4$ lb	=	120g
8 oz	=	$^1/_2$ lb	=	240g
12 oz	=	$^3/_4$ lb	=	360g
16 oz	=	1 lb	=	480g

USEFUL EQUIVALENTS FOR LENGTH

To convert inches to centimeters, multiply number of inches by 2.5

1 in				=	2.5 cm		
6 in	=	$^1/_2$ ft		=	15 cm		
12 in	=	1 ft		=	30 cm		
36 in	=	3 ft	=	1 yd	=	90 cm	
40 in				=	100 cm	=	1 m

USEFUL EQUIVALENTS FOR COOKING/OVEN TEMPERATURES

	Fahrenheit		Celsius		Gas Mark
Freeze Water	32° F	=	0° C		
Room Temperature	68° F	=	20° C		
Boil Water	212° F	=	100° C		
Bake	325° F	=	160° C	=	3
	350° F	=	180° C	=	4
	375° F	=	190° C	=	5
	400° F	=	200° C	=	6
	425° F	=	220° C	=	7
	450° F	=	230° C	=	8
Broil				=	Grill

USEFUL EQUIVALENTS FOR LIQUID INGREDIENTS BY VOLUME

$^1/_4$ tsp							=	1 ml
$^1/_2$ tsp							=	2 ml
1 tsp							=	5 ml
3 tsp	=	1 tbls			=	$^1/_2$ fl oz	=	15 ml
		2 tbls	=	$^1/_8$ cup	=	1 fl oz	=	30 ml
		4 tbls	=	$^1/_4$ cup	=	2 fl oz	=	60 ml
		5$^1/_3$ tbls	=	$^1/_3$ cup	=	3 fl oz	=	80 ml
		8 tbls	=	$^1/_2$ cup	=	4 fl oz	=	120 ml
		10$^2/_3$ tbls	=	$^2/_3$ cup	=	5 fl oz	=	160 ml
		12 tbls	=	$^3/_4$ cup	=	6 fl oz	=	180 ml
		16 tbls	=	1 cup	=	8 fl oz	=	240 ml
		1 pt	=	2 cups	=	16 fl oz	=	480 ml
		1 qt	=	4 cups	=	32 fl oz	=	960 ml
						33 fl oz	=	1000 ml (1 liter)

NOTES